THE COMPASSIONATE ENTREPRENEUR

Building an Ethical Business with Patience and Integrity that Lasts

Dr. Navdeep Chawla

STARDOM BOOKS

www.StardomBooks.com

STARDOM BOOKS
112 Bordeaux Ct.
Coppell, TX 75019, USA

FIRST EDITION FEBRUARY 2026

STARDOM BOOKS, LLC.
112 Bordeaux Ct. Coppell, TX 75019, USA

www.stardombooks.com

Stardom Books
United States and India

THE COMPASSIONATE ENTREPRENEUR

Building an Ethical Business with Patience and Integrity that Lasts

Dr. Navdeep Chawla

p. 216
cm. 13.97 X 21.59

Category : BUS025000 Business & Economics : Entrepreneurship
BUS107000 Business & Economics : Personal Success

ISBN : 978-1-957456-84-3

Dedication

This book is dedicated to my parents, who gave me the gift of dreams and the ability to realize them.

Acknowledgments

This book is as much yours as it is mine. To my family—for the countless conversations, gentle nudges and steadfast love that shaped not just these words, but the person I am.

Contents

Foreword — *i*

1. Unleashing The Entrepreneurial Mindset — *1*

2. The Art of Waiting — *15*

3. Resisting The Rush — *33*

4. The Honest Enterprise — *49*

5. Ethics In Business — *65*

6. Fair Play — *79*

7. When To Pass the Baton — *97*

8. Training The Next Generation of Leaders — *127*

9. Giving Back — *157*

10. The Long Road to Balance — *179*

Conclusion — *193*

About the Author — *199*

Foreword

"The purpose of life is not to be happy. It is to be useful, to be honorable, to be compassionate... to have it make some difference that you have lived and lived well."

— Ralph Waldo Emerson

Unlike what some others might claim, I did not build my business overnight. My journey began with more humble roots—the start of a small printing press just after graduation. I later joined CIBA-GEIGY, where I spent seven years learning the intricacies of the pharmaceutical industry. In 1986, I took the leap and founded my own company, Psychotropics India Ltd.

What started as a small endeavor has now grown into a global pharmaceutical business, with operations spanning over 50 countries. We supply to leading government and private institutions, including AIIMS, the Indian Army, and Indian Railways, as well as to prominent corporate hospitals in India, such as the Medanta Group, Paras Group, Shalby Hospitals, and many more.

I have witnessed firsthand the rise and fall of companies' mistakes that can bring down even the most promising ventures, and strategies that ensure long-term success.

Beyond business, I have dedicated my time to various leadership roles—serving as the President of the Faridabad Industry Association, contributing to educational institutions, and spearheading numerous charitable initiatives. I can confidently say these experiences have shaped my understanding of business, leadership, and the responsibility that comes with success.

This book is not just theory—it is a distillation of decades of real-world experience, both my own and that of the countless entrepreneurs I have worked with and learned from. I hope that by sharing these lessons, I can help you build a business that not only grows but thrives with integrity and resilience.

The Illusion of Overnight Success

In the world of business, we are often fed stories of dazzling overnight successes. The media loves to celebrate young entrepreneurs who seem to emerge from nowhere, landing million-dollar deals, launching game-changing startups, and reaching levels of success that others may take decades to achieve. But beneath the glossy headlines, the reality is far different. For every so-called overnight success, there is a foundation of years—sometimes decades—of hard work, patience, and strategic decision-making. The truth? There is no such thing as an overnight success. It is a myth that sets unrealistic expectations and leads countless entrepreneurs to frustration, burnout, and failure.

I have seen both sides of the entrepreneurial journey—those who sprinted toward success only to burn out too quickly, and those who played the long game, building businesses with integrity, strategy, and patience. If there is one lesson I have learned over the decades, it is this: sustainable success requires patience, honesty, and the wisdom to know when to push forward and when to step back.

The Entrepreneur's Struggle: Why This Matters to You

Every entrepreneur, regardless of industry, faces a common set of struggles. The pressure to grow rapidly, outpace competitors, secure funding, and achieve quick wins often prompts business leaders to make short-term decisions that compromise long-term sustainability.

Many fall into the trap of overpromising and underdelivering, cutting ethical corners, or exhausting themselves in the relentless pursuit of immediate success.

But what if success wasn't about how fast you could achieve it? What if instead it was about how well you could sustain it? What if the real secret to business wasn't velocity, but vision?

This book is an invitation to step away from the relentless race and instead build something that lasts—a business built on trust, ethical competition, and the wisdom of knowing when to hold on and when to let go.

This is not a book about shortcuts or hacks to instant wealth. It is a book about patience, about playing the long game, about building businesses that not only succeed momentarily but also endure for generations.

This book is divided into ten chapters, each exploring a critical element of entrepreneurial longevity.

- Chapter 1 reframes the entrepreneurial journey as a marathon, not a sprint—where patience becomes a core strategy, not just a virtue.
- Chapter 2 uncovers the quiet strength behind iconic success stories, spotlighting how long-term thinking shaped industry leaders.
- Chapter 3 explores how managing expectations and emotional pressure is vital to building with clarity rather than chasing chaos.
- Chapter 4 focuses on honesty as a business foundation—showing how transparency builds trust, loyalty, and operational harmony.

- Chapter 5 positions ethics as a competitive advantage, illustrating how integrity leads to sustainable growth and strong reputations.
- Chapter 6 examines the power of fair play in competitive spaces and how businesses can win without compromising their values.
- Chapter 7 reflects on the importance of timing your exit—planning succession that honors both the founder's journey and the future.
- Chapter 8 delves into leadership development and highlights mentorship as key to nurturing values-aligned future decision-makers.
- Chapter 9 expands the entrepreneurial purpose—encouraging founders to use their platforms for community, impact, and service.
- Chapter 10 ties it all together, emphasizing the need for balance, foresight, and continuous reflection to build a meaningful legacy.

By the end of this book, you will have gained insights into:

1. Understanding why true success is built over time, not in a rush.
2. How honesty, transparency, and ethical leadership create long-term brand loyalty.
3. Learning how patience can help you navigate business uncertainties without compromising your mental and emotional well-being.
4. How to rise above cut-throat business practices and create an enterprise that competes with integrity.
5. Recognizing when to step back, mentor the next generation, and ensure the legacy of your work continues.

Each chapter offers real-world examples, practical strategies, and lessons drawn from some of the biggest successes—and failures—in the business world. Whether you are just starting out or have years of experience, this book will challenge the way you think about entrepreneurship and success.

What This Book Is—And What It Isn't

This book is not about quick-fix strategies or get-rich-quick schemes. It does not promise overnight success or tell you that you need to work 20 hours a day to build a fortune. Instead, it is a guide to sustainable success—one that values patience, ethical decision-making, and long-term vision over short-term gains.

If you are looking for a blueprint to build a life and business that lasts, if you believe that integrity and success are not mutually exclusive, and if you are ready to commit to a journey that prioritizes wisdom over haste, then this book is for you.

However, if you are searching for a magic formula to skyrocket your business overnight, this is not the book for you. Sustainable success requires effort, strategy, and, above all, time.

Are You Ready for the Journey?

The trail is not meant for those who sprint recklessly—it is for those who strategize, plan, and move forward with purpose.

This book is your invitation to shift your perspective—to see entrepreneurship not as a race to the finish line but as a carefully navigated journey.

In the next chapter, we'll begin this journey by exploring the entrepreneurial mindset—how patience, vision, and resilience shape the foundation of a truly successful business. Let's take that first step together.

1

Unleashing the Entrepreneurial Mindset

A Journey beyond velocity

"Most people overestimate what they can do in one year and underestimate what they can do in ten years."

— Bill Gates

Embarking on the entrepreneurial journey is not just a leap into the unknown; it's a thrilling adventure brimming with excitement and potential. It's like setting sail on a vast ocean, not knowing what lies beyond the horizon. You've come here with ambition, inspired by the tales of a land of bounty. You arrived with the idea of success, eager to break from the mediocrity you once lived in. This run led you to a challenging situation; the question you might encounter is, what's next?

This situation might seem daunting at first, like staring into an abyss. However, the more you analyze the problem, the more opportunities you see.

For instance, when I started my first company, I faced the challenge of finding the right market for my product.

I had to conduct market research and adapt my products to meet customer needs. The point of this analogy is that the entrepreneurial journey is about discovering hidden opportunities through patient investigation. The fruits of your labor come with consistency over time.

Imagine your entrepreneurial journey as a game of golf. Just like in golf, your journey will have its highs and lows. Unexpected changes may come your way, and your ability to adapt to these changes can turn the tide of the journey in your favor. The key is to embrace the changes and make the most of them, using them as stepping stones to your success. It's like playing a game where you  must be flexible and quickly respond to changes to win. You must endure the tough times to achieve success. It's more like a long-drawn match of ever-changing strategies. Like in golf, you can only let up at the last minute. It's common in golf for the previous shot to change the outcome of the results. So, like in golf, the idea is to always keep at it, without letting a blind spot take advantage of your position. You have to maintain consistency in your determination towards the goal.

As the saying goes, *"It is not worth comparing the sufferings you are to face in the present to the glory you will face in the future."* This idea is essential in life and in building your company from the ground up.

In your journey, you will face many tough decisions to uphold, and in the long run, you will have to act on them. But you will succeed if you are disciplined toward your goal and persevere through the challenges. In other words, don't give up when things get tough. Keep your eyes on the prize and keep moving forward.

It's a strong idea since you can only achieve your ideal success if you know where you want to end up. Often, entrepreneurs chase a flimsy idea of being rich or famous, but that is not quantifiable.

Because if you chase a goal like that, where do you draw the line and say you've made it? Where do you hold the tape and say you've crossed it? That's what happens when you chase something like that, since nothing is ever enough.

Before I entered the pharmaceutical industry, my entrepreneurial journey started with a very small printing press. It was a challenging yet fulfilling experience, with very long hours. But the joy of seeing the final product made it worthwhile. After that, I worked for esteemed companies like CIBA-GEIGY (now Novartis) and Themis Chemicals Limited. These experiences gave me the knowledge and insights necessary to establish a successful presence in the pharmaceutical field.

In my experience with my first company and the companies I later joined, I realized that I wasn't pursuing vague goals like making money. If money had been my priority, I would have been content with my salary at Novartis or Themis. Instead, I envisioned what I wanted to build and established it.

Now, you might need help to succeed. However, once you get the money, you might lose the ambition to keep at it. We often see this on 'Shark Tank,' a popular TV show where entrepreneurs pitch their business ideas to a panel of investors. These companies sometimes receive massive investments but end up being run to the ground because the entrepreneur heading the operation went off with the money. This is why it's important to know what your goal is. For instance, look at the success story of Elon Musk, who started with a vision of revolutionizing the transportation industry and is now leading companies like Tesla and SpaceX. His clear goal and strategic planning have been key to his success.

The essence of entrepreneurial success lies in the understanding that it's not an overnight journey. It's akin to hunting; a skilled hunter spends days observing the terrain, learning the animal's tracks and behavior patterns. Over time, the hunter positions themselves, aims, and shoots. As the age-old adage goes, Rome wasn't built in a day. The greatness of Rome was the result of years of vision, planning, and painstaking effort. Brick by brick, road by road, system by system—it evolved into a civilization admired for its strength and structure. The message is clear: no matter the end goal, something of significant magnitude cannot be rushed. It all requires patience and perseverance. So, in your entrepreneurial journey, take the time to observe, learn, and position yourself for success.

Patience is essential for success. Through enduring trials, you learn the necessary steps to reach your goals, and time is your best teacher. As time passes, you will understand the lessons you need and recognize your strengths and weaknesses. Over time, you will learn what helps you succeed and what brings you down. These lessons will guide your future actions.

You are more likely to have support if you have a well-thought-out plan. Understanding the concept of time also helps maintain composure and discern between emotions and ambition. Why does this matter, you might wonder? When building a company, you'll need to make many sacrifices. That's why you can't cling to every aspect of the original plan and expect it to survive unharmed.

To simplify, think of it as a puzzle. You need a clear vision of the end goal, and then you can assemble the pieces until the entire picture is finished.

Debunking The Quick Success Myth

Success always comes at a price. The hard-earned achievements of prodigies like Steve Jobs and Mark Zuckerberg are often misunderstood as strokes of luck. Their status as university dropouts is frequently misinterpreted by misinformed youth as a shortcut to success. However, the truth is that when Steve Jobs and Mark Zuckerberg dropped out, they both had a vision and purpose that they were deeply passionate about.

Mark Zuckerberg was a prodigy at programming, and his overnight success at Facebook came with hours of coding through trial and error. He could do this because of years of coding practice, learning, and interaction that preceded that moment. We see a similar idea with Steve Jobs: his charisma made millions for Apple, but that cannot be as true as they think. The truth is that the company wouldn't make a cent if it had nothing to offer. The idea of charisma comes when you know the horse you're backing is reliable, and that was the case with Steve Jobs. He couldn't engineer the components, but he knew what he foresaw. Many people say Steve Wozniak built Apple. However, when you look at it from what it is, Steve Jobs was there with Steve Wozniak in that group, who had worked on it for years in the earlier system to put it together. So, nothing comes with having a good smile in a matter of minutes. You have to struggle to reach the top of the stairs to success. Additionally, even the concept of quantifiable success is flexible. The point of success loses its reasonable foundation or meaning. This means what we do often could be the spitting image of uninspired at best.

The second point is almost like rebellion, where one confronts life's challenges and uses them as motivation. This can be understood through a quote from psychologist and philosopher Jordan B. Peterson: "The only way out is through. You take the thing that poisons you until you turn it into the tonic that girdles the world around you." This concept drives forward that life can feel like hell when one is in a difficult situation.

However, sometimes, the only way out of suffering with a reward for your labor is to go headfirst. In addition, you must see and understand the things holding you back. Study it and find out the cause and effect. Often, what holds you back can help you flourish and take a far greater stance in your field. You can find a way to outsource your troubleshooting to other systems, which can generate additional revenue. Simultaneously, you can learn from the systems you're helping to troubleshoot, giving you a database of how to deal with other problems.

With this, you will find that you will change not only your system but many different systems, not only in the work you put in, but also in how others perceive you. They will become your ally instead of looking at you as a threat. You take what burdens you might face and turn them into something that helps you in the long run.

That is the point of the long game. Your returns will be similar to the work you put in. You must know that you will not be successful just by imagining things. One day of effort will not make you a billionaire like Jeff Bezos, who didn't wake up and dream up the idea for Amazon, nor did Elon Musk do the same with Tesla.

The concepts were developed with considerable feedback and errors in the initial phases. In some cases, they started with a whole different idea and a whole different company. As you look at the history of Amazon, it was a whole other system from what it is today.

Like Tesla, the company began as a novelty brand for rich tech enthusiasts.

These companies are an example of a situation where you sometimes don't know what will make you a success story. You put the work in, and suddenly, when your chips are down, you will look up to see your magnum opus. The fact that you have the idea that you want to be an entrepreneur means that you want to leave your mark on this world.

One way for the team to embrace the position you place them in is to understand them, know their work, and be aware of their ambitions. Many of my employees had aspirations to build their empires, so we allowed them to do so to forge a partnership with us in the long run rather than becoming adversarial toward the entire organization.

I asked about their family's ambitions and helped those who wanted to pursue higher education. We also supported the wives of many employees in obtaining their B.Ed. Degrees and helped them secure jobs, providing an additional source of income for their families. This has helped us build strong relationships with our employees, which in turn has boosted morale.

As an employee at Themis Chemicals, I dreamed of making my mark in the market. This drove me away from the security of being under someone else and motivated me to take the adventure of entrepreneurship myself.

Decision-Making Without Strategic Thinking

The thought of building anything must come with a strategic plan, as you need to know what you do, where, and how. Many of you might know this: as with building a house, you don't just construct on sand.

Instead, you would have to dig through the stone and build your foundation, which you would inspect again to ensure it's not shaky. After that, you would use the best material to build the house's skeletal frame. And only then will you make your home its ideal form. Just as with the house, you must work on building your business. You cannot cut corners to save time or reap the reward before you finish constructing. If you do that to a house, it will not be able to withstand the rough weather. What do you think will happen to a poorly developed business?

One common problem with a rushed approach is the tendency to overlook better decisions. At first, it may seem as though you've achieved success with quick, superficial solutions. But beneath the surface lie undercurrents that can eventually derail your efforts. It's similar to the early explorers—some maps charted the visible routes, currents, and tides, but missed the deeper, hidden forces that truly shaped the journey.

Let's consider a situation where the ship is at risk if it continues on its current path. If the captain acts hastily without consulting the navigator, the crew might initially praise the captain. However, they would need to find out where this new course would take them. This is similar to running a business. It would help if you planned to predict the outcomes of a situation. Taking action without careful consideration can lead to more stress and lower team morale, resulting in reduced efficiency. The key is to anticipate the potential outcomes of our actions as accurately as possible. By doing so, we can identify mistakes and develop solutions to them.

The benefit of analyzing every move is that you can learn from many other experiences that came before you. This would mean you can see how things pan out with most moves, causing you to see the outcomes unfurl before you.

This will make you wiser about what to expect. While being efficient is essential, being hasty in your decisions can lead to numerous missed opportunities. Entrepreneurs often rush to launch their product in the market. But doing so usually leaves little room for proper research and development, which weakens the product. This, in turn, opens the door for competitors to step in with a stronger launch.

If you have a product similar to existing ones in the market, it would be beneficial to see how established competitors fare in the market and make the necessary quality improvements. These opportunities come when you have time to think before taking action. Remember the quote by Maxime Lagace: *"Wisdom starts when you no longer need short-term rewards."* The lure of quick returns can be tempting, but it often pushes you into playing the worst hand, leading to bigger losses in the long run. This impatience is common in younger approaches—it shows eagerness, which is good, but eagerness without caution can cause avoidable mistakes.

Along that line, rushed decisions can cause one to lose alignment with one's moral base or the main idea behind one's goal. Minor hurried decisions could also lead one off the trajectory of their goals or projections. When things don't go as planned, you often end up spending more effort realigning yourself than you did making the decision that threw you off course.

Decisions like this are often precarious since a company's foundation is built on many factors. As the analogy with building a house goes, if the structure at the top gets damaged, it can be mended. However, the foundation cannot withstand the same abuse.

Every hasty move forces the company to rechart much of its carefully laid plans just to keep the system stable. This doesn't bode well for the company.

With such rushed moves, stakeholders often end up neglected, and the company is left putting out fires instead of moving forward.

This kind of misstep can make both you and your team lose focus on what truly matters—the stakeholders. When that happens, the board may begin to lose faith in your performance, and in some cases, in your entire operation, which can ultimately cost you financial backing. That is why it is paramount to ensure that every move is well thought out. You cannot afford to alienate the very people investing in your dreams.

The plan is to work in a way that aligns with the system you're operating in, ensuring it runs efficiently and with minimal risk. When you rush, however, you create more fires than you can put out. As one fire is being doused, another ignites, and soon the process slows to a snail's pace under the weight of constant crisis management.

In my company, many rushed decisions seemed like the right choice. However, diving into foolish mistakes could have been detrimental to our business. It would have been like building my castle on unstable ground. We would have had to compromise the integrity of the company we built, which we were not willing to do. We have reached our current position because of careful planning and thoughtful consideration.

While working at CIBA-GEIGY, we were encouraged to uphold good values, particularly honest and ethical market practices. It was crucial for us to maintain integrity, even in the face of our competitors' underhanded practices.

Although this ethos may seem outdated in today's cutthroat market, honesty is fundamental in building trust and reliability.

The Benefits of A Long-Term Perspective

Thinking long-term can help you take a more relaxed approach to your situation. It's similar to a football coach who studies the opponent's strategies before the match and then briefs the team on what to do and when. This planning helps the players prepare for every variation of the opponent's moves.

This approach eliminates last-minute scrambling to secure a win in the match, allowing the team to work steadily and efficiently.

Additionally, it provides a clearer vision of success, leading to more victories. This is what a business should focus on when strategizing. Doing so will establish a clearer path, enabling the enterprise to move in a predictable direction.

Just because a path is predictable doesn't make it bad. Rather, it is a good sign since it means you know the difficulties that will arise and can maneuver around them. These scenes of predictability can also lead to strategic advantage since you know what you're looking for.

Think of the Titanic. The tragedy only happened because of the iceberg's low visibility, leading the ship to turn too late. Predictability should not be considered monotone or something that has lost its spice when no disaster occurs. In fact, predictability in business is like the white flag in a Grand Prix race: it signals that things are moving smoothly toward a safe close.

For a business, this steadiness makes difficult times more bearable. It also builds confidence—both in your leadership and in the process itself—among investors. You will also have more people lining up to invest in you. This will strengthen your position in the long run, especially given your thoughtful approach to running the business. This will also have goodwill with other high-position members since they would be more open to a businessman with his head on his shoulders than a brash, action-oriented fool.

This is also because, often, these people have a vested interest in seeing your business bloom. Because of this, they might expect you to be somewhat responsible.

Making your mark is a lot easier if you are consistent; consistency, in the long run, makes you better than yesterday. It's like sports; in any sport, if you are consistent with one technique or one skill and master it to perfection, you can win any contest with it. The same goes for business.

The only difference is that in sports, you are sought after because of your untapped potential, and in business, you are sought after when you show promise with prior evidence to back it up. Keeping a long-term mindset—reminding yourself that 'practice makes me better than yesterday'—can work wonders. This mindset proves valuable in many situations, especially when you're looking to generate interest and investment in your ideas, because stability naturally attracts investors.

Establishing my pharmaceutical venture under the brand name Psychotropics India Limited was challenging. Some situations would have caused anyone in my position to take shortcuts for quick success. When manufacturing prescription drugs, we had to deal with a dishonest practice where rival companies would bribe doctors with trips to Europe and other freebies. However, with a determined mindset and patient thinking, we succeeded through ethical methods.

Patience In Fostering Creative Thinking

Being patient is pivotal for long-term success in business. It goes back to sports, which is about building yourself up. The idea is that real progress comes from steady, consistent effort over time. Small, sustained actions compound into meaningful results.

In contrast, pouring in excessive effort all at once can overwhelm you, causing fatigue or burnout. Instead of moving you forward, it can backfire and break your momentum. Similarly, in business, minor, well-thought-out improvements can lead to success in the gradual sense.

Over time, there is a greater likelihood of discovery, which could lead to more revenue streams or the discovery of a new troubleshooting system. The idea is that persistence leads to good fruit.

A great case study of this idea of patience is the story of Ariana Huffington. Her company is now popularly known as the Huffington Post. Her brand's work is well-received, but its success didn't happen overnight. Rather, it was built over trial and error, making her achieve widespread popularity. The point of persistence comes with her attempts to establish her position in the market. Initially, she was interested in becoming an author. However, her attempts led her to be rejected by over thirty-six different publishing houses. This led her to discover that there was a need for a publishing house, which led her to start her own and become the success she is now.

The concept of patience also applies to building your team. Many entrepreneurs make the mistake of shouldering the entire burden of the company themselves. They fail to delegate because they are always looking for quick results. When you delegate, you exercise the chain of command, allowing team members to give external ideas.

I normally delegate to have a capable team by my side. That is what happens when you are patient with the outcome rather than working solely on making a profit and focusing on building a team of employees. You will be on top of the situation regardless.

For example, the employees who later left the company returned as partners with their system, and we partnered with them.

Just as I delegated the responsibility of building the infrastructure to the technocrats, we were able to outperform others in the market. That decision not only helped us establish our mark but also led to profitability.

This is why delegation is not just useful—it is essential. Instead of bearing the burden of research and development on my own, they made the most of it. This makes the employees feel like you have faith in their capacities.

In the end, success is rarely about speed alone. It is about patience, careful planning, and the courage to trust others with responsibility. Rushing may give you the illusion of progress, but only steadiness builds something that lasts.

2

The Art of Waiting

"The two most powerful warriors are patience and time."
— Leo Tolstoy

I n a world where 'now' is often too late, success stories are often painted as overnight triumphs. But the reality? The greatest businesses and most impactful innovations are built on patience. This chapter is about the endurance behind those so-called 'instant' successes, reminding us that the most substantial wins come to those who are willing to wait, adapt, and persist.

Patience in business isn't about sitting back and waiting for things to happen—it's about making strategic decisions, nurturing talent, and embracing calculated risks that unfold over time.

Now, here's the thing—growth in any organization is next to impossible without being driven by technology. But for a startup like ours, where there was no finance, no investors lining up, and no deep pockets to fund R&D, we couldn't even think about integrating technology unless we were brilliant.

When I started my business, I knew one thing: growth without technology was not possible. But unlike tech-driven startups with deep pockets and investor backing, we had none of that. We weren't a Silicon Valley venture founded by coding geniuses. We were marketeers, salespeople, and problem-solvers, navigating an industry where innovation required more than just ambition—it required execution. We had no in-house research team, no expensive R&D lab, and no budget for cutting-edge technological advancements.

So, what did we have?

We had our thought process. We had our collective experience in sales and marketing. And we had a hunger to innovate. But we also knew that without technology, we couldn't scale. The challenge was clear: how do we integrate technology into our business when we lack the infrastructure and resources to support it?

Creating a Technological Edge Without Capital

Quite early on in our journey, we realized that manufacturing generic medicines was not going to give us an edge. The margins were slim, competition was cutthroat, and there was no significant differentiation. If we wanted to break through, we needed an edge— something that would allow us to carve out a niche in a crowded market. We needed to diversify into high-tech products that could command a market premium. That's when we decided to explore the idea of manufacturing sustained-release or delayed-release pharmaceutical products in the year of 1993.

To put it simply, let's take the example of an antihistamine like Advil. If you take a standard tablet, its effect lasts about eight hours, which means you need to take another dose three times a day to maintain the desired effect.

But what if we could develop a formulation that releases the drug gradually, extending the effect to 12 hours? That would mean the patient only needs to take the medicine twice a day—once in the morning and once at night—offering not just better convenience but also improved compliance. We had the vision, but we lacked the technology to make it a reality.

Thinking Beyond Conventional R&D

With no R&D team and no funding for expensive scientific and pharmaceutical consultation, we had to think outside the box. So, we got creative. I scoured the internet, did my research, and finally discovered a group of retired European scientists eager to support emerging companies. These were experts who had spent decades in pharmaceutical research but were now looking for opportunities to contribute their knowledge—not for money, but for the experience of exploring new countries and cultures. I reached out to them with a simple proposition: come to India, work with us, train our team in advanced pharmaceutical techniques, and in return, we will host you, take care of your travel, and give you an opportunity to explore the country. We would take them to the Taj Mahal in Agra, tourist landmarks in Jaipur, and other historic sites in India, offering them all-expenses-paid holidays for 15 days. For us, the cost was minimal compared to what hiring full-time consultants or setting up a high-end research lab would have entailed. And for them, it was an exciting and fulfilling opportunity. This unconventional approach paid off. Not only did we develop a highly effective sustained-release anti-allergic drug (antihistamine)—the first of its kind in the country—but we also built internal expertise that allowed us to replicate this innovation across different drug categories. And that's where our next breakthrough happened.

Breaking Into the Anti-Diabetic Market

Diabetes management is all about maintaining consistent blood sugar levels. When diabetic patients had to take their medication every six to eight hours, it often led to missed doses and inconsistent treatment. With our newly acquired expertise, we leveraged the sustained-release technology; we formulated drugs that could extend the release of the active ingredient for 12 hours. This meant that instead of taking three doses a day, patients could simply take one tablet in the morning with breakfast and another at night with dinner. This not only improved adherence to the medication but also significantly enhanced patient convenience, making treatment significantly more manageable.

By innovating in this space, we not only differentiated ourselves but also positioned our company as an early leader in the anti-diabetic segment. Today, our generic sustained-release formulations are among the best-selling in the industry.

The lesson? Technology is indispensable. But when resources are scarce, innovation isn't just about what you create—it's about how you bring expertise into your company without breaking the bank.

Lessons in Growth and Adaptability

Technology, in my experience, is a fundamental driver of success, almost like a non-negotiable factor in business growth. Large corporations have the luxury of building state-of-the-art R&D teams, but for startups, the challenge isn't just about having money—it's about being resourceful. It's about finding unconventional ways to tap into knowledge, expertise, and creativity. By integrating technology and empowering the right people, you can build systems that are both efficient and sustainable.

Looking back, our decision to leverage external expertise while keeping costs minimal was one of the smartest moves we made. It reinforced a key lesson: when resources are limited, creativity and adaptability become your most valuable assets.

Funding was another mountain to climb. Today, all kinds of investors dole out money to promising startups. But two decades ago, no such opportunities existed. We had ideas, demand was growing, but we had no capital to scale. The government had no policies to support small enterprises with unsecured loans. Every rupee had to be backed by tangible assets—land, property, securities.

I still remember the year 1989, standing in my banker's office, hoping for a loan. He asked, "Mr. Chawla, what security do you have?"

"Nothing," I admitted.

"No property? No commercial assets?"

"No."

"Any life insurance policies?" he pressed.

That caught my attention. "Yes."

"National Savings Certificates?"

"Yes, but I don't know their worth."

He agreed to meet me after banking hours at six in the evening. The next day, I gathered all my insurance policies and savings certificates. The grand total? ₹1,20,000.

"I can loan you 75% of this," he said. So, my total worth in 1989 was ₹90,000.

I grabbed the offer. I signed every document he put before me, assigned my policies, and walked out with a loan that would change the course of my business.

Why do I remember that moment so vividly? Because today, we negotiate loans of ₹40–50 crore on our own terms.

But back then, the power was entirely in the bank's hands. The journey from pleading for a few lakhs to commanding multimillion-dollar deals is what patience and perseverance look like. Many entrepreneurs fail because they rush. They take their first big paycheck and buy a luxury car instead of reinvesting in their business.

They inflate their lifestyles before stabilizing their finances. That is a fatal mistake. First-generation entrepreneurs must move slowly and steadily—every step measured; every decision calculated.

But the greatest strength of any business isn't funding or technology—it's people. Entrepreneurs who think they know everything set themselves up for failure. Leadership isn't about dictating decisions; it's about hiring the right people and trusting them to build the company alongside you.

I believe in hiring the best, even if it costs a little more. I can't afford an IIM or Harvard graduate, but I can develop my talents. When you nurture employees, give them ownership, and build them into leaders, they become the backbone of your business.

Over time, your company forms an ecosystem—one leader in technology, another in finance, another in marketing, administration, HR, and so on. This isn't just a company anymore; it's a self-sustaining entity.

And learning never stops. Entrepreneurs can't afford 10-day training courses at elite institutions. But we can attend industry seminars, network with experts, and sit with consultants over tea. The best knowledge often comes from conversations, from understanding the pulse of the market, and from surrounding ourselves with people who know more than we do.

Every entrepreneur's journey is unique, but the foundations of success remain universal—embrace technology, secure smart funding, build a formidable team, and never stop learning.

Mastering the Art of Waiting

There are a few towering examples in Indian business history—leaders whose patience, perseverance, and vision have built empires that stand strong even today. Cipla, for instance, is one of the best examples. Before Partition, K.A. Hamied laid the foundation of Cipla, and today, nearly a century later, Dr. Yusuf Hamied continues to be the guiding force behind the company, even while being based in London. His contributions to transforming Cipla into a global pharmaceutical powerhouse are nothing short of legendary.

Then, there is the story of Hero Group, an empire that started with bicycles and went on to dominate the motorcycle industry. Brijmohan Lall Munjal, the man behind this success, is a name that should never be forgotten. His journey from assembling bicycles in a modest workshop in Ludhiana to building one of the world's largest two-wheeler manufacturers is a testament to patience, strategy, and an unwavering commitment to relationships.

I recall an incident that left a deep impression on me. Once, while visiting a city in Rajasthan, I met a pharma distributor who also happened to be a major cycle distributor. Over a casual conversation, he said, "Mr. Chawla, it's quite a coincidence that we work with your company, and we have also worked with Hero Cycles for years. Mr. Munjal, like you, hails from Ludhiana." Intrigued, I asked him what it was like working with such a titan. His response stayed with me. "Mr. Munjal had over 2,000 distributors across the country," he said, "and yet, every time he visited me, he remembered the names of my children, asked about my wife, and inquired about the very problem I had shared with him in our last meeting. He made me feel valued— not just as a business partner, but as a part of the Hero family. That connection was so strong that, to this day, I have never allowed a competitor to enter my cycle business."

That story changed my perspective on leadership. I realized that a business is not just built on numbers; it thrives on relationships. Inspired by this, we introduced a similar practice in our company. We started conducting family meetings within our distribution network. Rather than visiting every distributor individually, we began hosting annual gatherings—one in Rajasthan, another in Punjab, another in Maharashtra—where all our key distributors and their families would come together. We would not just discuss business strategies and future plans, but we would also celebrate with them—spend an evening in a beautiful resort, share meals, exchange stories, and truly connect. Even today, we continue this tradition, which has helped me personally know at least 40-50% of my key customers. More than that, it has reinforced the idea that patience, relationships, and genuine interest in people's lives create the strongest foundation for long-term success. Learning, as I always say, never ends.

As entrepreneurs, we must always keep our eyes open—not just to financial opportunities but also to the values and practices that make businesses timeless. Whether it is Cipla's relentless commitment to making medicines affordable or Hero Group's unwavering focus on nurturing relationships, there is something to learn from every great leader. The art of waiting, when coupled with wisdom and perseverance, is what truly separates a business that merely exists from one that leaves a lasting legacy.

Patience...Patience, What Patience?

Patience in business is not just a virtue—it is the bedrock on which enduring enterprises are built. For an entrepreneur who is truly self-made, without the cushion of inherited wealth or a safety net of financial backing, patience is not an option; it is the only way forward.

Look at my company; We created an ecosystem of reliability. We built an organization with a strong foundation, structured on discipline, integrity, and a cohesive team. Over time, we cultivated an impeccable reputation—one where financial institutions, investors, and stakeholders had absolute confidence in us. And that is the essence of patience—it is not just about waiting but about building.

Imagine constructing a pyramid. If you attempt to erect its peak before laying a solid base, it will collapse under its own weight. Businesses that chase instant success, that sprint before they can walk, often crumble because they lack foundational strength. The impatience to grow too fast, to expand without stability, is a recipe for failure. True business success is a steady climb—one where each layer of the pyramid is carefully placed, cemented with experience, resilience, and strategic foresight.

Patience is not passive; it is an active strategy. It involves the incubation of ideas—allowing them to mature, evolve, and align with the market rather than forcing them into premature execution. It is about nurturing talent—not just hiring the best people, but mentoring them, giving them space to develop their skills, and fostering leadership within the organization. A sustainable business is built when employees are empowered, not just instructed; when decisions are measured, not impulsive; and when growth is structured, not chaotic.

Many young entrepreneurs today look at success stories and only see the final result. They see towering enterprises, not the slow and grueling ascent that built them. But behind every industry leader, there is a story of patience—a period of struggle, of refining ideas, of making mistakes and learning from them. Patience is not about delaying success; it is about ensuring it is lasting. The greatest companies, the most respected leaders, and the most innovative enterprises have all mastered this art—the art of waiting, of perfecting, of enduring. That is how legacies are built.

One of the most compelling examples of patience in business is the story of Sun Pharma. When examining their product range, I noticed that they primarily focus on the chronic segment—medications required for chronic conditions. In contrast, many pharmaceutical companies specialize in anti-infectives, which are used for short durations. For example, if a patient has a throat infection, they take antibiotics for five days, and then the association with the medicine and the company ends.

However, chronic illnesses like hypertension and diabetes require lifelong medication. This strategic focus on the chronic segment allowed Sun Pharma to build a stable and long-lasting relationship with its customers. I recall attending a closed-door meeting where Dilip Shanghvi, the chairman of Sun Pharma, was asked why the company never ventured into antibiotics, vitamins, or nutritional supplements. His response was insightful. He asked a participant about the health conditions within his family. The participant mentioned that, while he did not take any medication, his older brother had hypertension, his sister had diabetes, and his parents had various chronic conditions requiring regular medication. Sanghvi explained that a pharmaceutical company's journey with a consumer typically begins at age 40 and above. By focusing on chronic conditions, Sun Pharma ensured that once a patient started using their products, they would continue to do so for life. This long-term vision required patience, but it ultimately led to sustained success.

Another noteworthy example is Mankind Pharma. Their initial strategy was simple but effective: they introduced medicines at almost half the price of market leaders. This made them highly competitive and allowed them to capture a significant market share.

However, as their business matured and competition increased, they realized the need to diversify and de-risk their operations. Over the years, they strategically expanded beyond pharmaceuticals into high-demand, over-the-counter (OTC) products.

One of their most successful ventures was in the contraceptive market. They launched "Manforce" Condoms, which became the leading brand in India. At the time, condom advertisements were restricted to post-9 PM television slots. They capitalized on this by featuring top Bollywood actresses in their campaigns, making the product highly visible and desirable. This clever marketing, combined with a strong distribution network, propelled Manforce to the number one position in the industry.

Mankind Pharma didn't stop there. They further expanded into diagnostic services by launching Pathkind Labs, establishing a presence in the growing pathology and diagnostic testing industry. Most recently, they acquired Bharat Serums Limited, a company specializing in vaccines.

Vaccines, unlike pharmaceuticals, are administered only a few times in a person's life, making them a distinct yet complementary segment. By entering this space, Mankind Pharma strategically diversified its portfolio while staying within the broader healthcare ecosystem. Their ability to pivot and explore new opportunities demonstrates how patience, coupled with strategic expansion, leads to long-term success.

Whether it was Sun Pharma's focus on chronic conditions or Mankind Pharma's calculated moves into OTC products and diagnostics, both companies exemplify how a patient approach, combined with smart business acumen, can yield extraordinary results.

The Power of Patience in Leadership

I've walked through the offices of countless entrepreneurs, watched them at work, observed their habits, their frustrations, and their successes. And time after time, I have seen the same pattern—business owners buried in paperwork, signing checks for hours, scrutinizing bills, and making rounds in their factories, only to spend the rest of their day yelling at their staff.

"This isn't done right!" "That's not how I told you to do it!" "Why is this taking so long?"

Their impatience filled the air, their frustration trickled down to their teams, creating an environment of fear rather than innovation. But then, I have also seen another kind of leader. One who steps back, watches, listens, and waits. One who empowers instead of controls.

When I was the President of the Faridabad Industries Association, I had the privilege of visiting many successful factories and businesses. It didn't take long to notice the stark difference. The companies that thrived weren't the ones where the owner was involved in every tiny detail. They were the ones where leadership had patience—where trust was built, teams were empowered, and ideas were given space to breathe.

I remember a time when I had to appoint a new manager. It should have been a simple decision, but I agonized over it.

How much authority should I give him? What if he makes a mistake? What if his decisions cost us money? The fear of loss, of things spiraling out of control, kept me up at night.

Then one evening, as I sat at my desk, a thought struck me—*How does Ratan Tataji do it?*

The Tata Group is a mammoth empire. They run everything from steel to software, cars to chemicals. Mr. Tata cannot possibly oversee every little decision across his businesses.

And yet, they function like well-oiled machines.

The answer was simple: he trusts his people. He picks the right leaders, gives them the tools to succeed, and lets them take ownership. He doesn't hover over their shoulders, waiting to correct their every move. Instead, he exercises patience, stepping in only when necessary.

That night, I made my decision. I delegated. I let go. And in doing so, I freed not just my manager, but myself.

Many business owners get caught in the trap of obsessing over profits, attending endless meetings, and micromanaging every decision. But the real secret to growth is patience—the ability to nurture talent, trust your team, and give ideas and time they need to flourish.

When you stop hovering, when you listen instead of lecturing, and when you allow creativity to flow freely, you don't just build a company—you build a legacy. Success in business is rarely a result of reckless ambition. It's built on patience, foresight, and understanding one's own strengths. Yet, time and again, we see entrepreneurs who, driven by impulse, chase grandeur without laying the groundwork.

Today, Tata is venturing into the complex world of semiconductor manufacturing—a completely new industry for them. But unlike Mallya, they aren't leaping blindly. They have partnered with the world's best technology firms. They have secured expertise, created an ecosystem, and ensured they have deep pockets to sustain losses before seeing profits.

That is the difference between patience and impulse.

Business is not a gamble. It's a calculated journey. Entering an unknown territory without preparation is like setting sail into a storm without a compass. It's not ambition that dooms entrepreneurs—it's the lack of patience to build, to plan, and to respect the process of success.

The Four Pillars of Organic Growth

Success in business is not a matter of luck or a single brilliant idea—it is a process of careful, patient construction. Many entrepreneurs make the mistake of rushing into expansion, eager to see quick results, only to find their businesses crumbling under the weight of poor preparation. Organic growth—the kind that is sustainable and truly transformative—requires patience and a strong foundation.

There are four key pillars that every business must establish to achieve significant growth.

1. The Right Team: People Build Businesses

The backbone of any company is its team. Without the right people, even the best ideas fail. When venturing into a new domain, entrepreneurs must ask themselves: *Do I have a team that understands this industry?* If not, the first step is to build one.

Take Vijay Mallya, for instance. When he decided to enter the airline business, did he have an experienced team of aviation experts guiding him? No. He built Kingfisher Airlines on branding and lifestyle appeal, but lacked the expertise required to navigate the cutthroat airline industry. In contrast, businesses that succeed in new ventures ensure they have the right minds in place before taking the leap.

2. Financial Preparedness: Growth Requires Fuel

No matter how ambitious an expansion plan is, it cannot take off without financial backing. Entrepreneurs must evaluate: *Are we generating enough profit to support this new direction?* If not, what funding options exist? A common mistake is assuming that debt is always accessible. But when a company's financials are weak, banks hesitate to lend. Many businesses then turn to private financing, often at exorbitant interest rates—sometimes as high as 3% per month.

This alone can bleed a business dry before it even sees returns.

A strong balance sheet makes it easier to secure loans at favorable rates, reducing the risk of financial strain.

3. Technology: The Competitive Edge

In today's business landscape, technology is not optional—it's a necessity. Whether a company develops its own technology, partners with an R&D team, or licenses it from others, innovation plays a crucial role in cost reduction, efficiency, and staying ahead of competitors. A business that scales without investing in technology eventually becomes obsolete. Entrepreneurs who recognize this take the time to integrate cutting-edge solutions before expanding, ensuring they remain competitive in their industry.

4. Strategic Planning: Execution is Everything

A brilliant idea with poor execution is just a wasted opportunity. Even with the right team, money, and technology, a business needs a well-thought-out plan. A key factor in execution is time management—a rushed plan with unrealistic deadlines is as dangerous as one that drags on indefinitely.

For instance, if an entrepreneur assumes they can sell and market a new product within two months but the reality of production logistics requires five months, they are setting themselves up for losses. Every delay causes financial strain, supply chain disruptions, and missed market opportunities. A carefully mapped-out plan with realistic timelines can prevent such failures.

These four pillars—team, financial strength, technology, and strategic execution—are the foundations of organic growth. Building them takes time, discipline, and patience. Entrepreneurs who recognize this are the ones who create legacies, not just short-lived successes. Businesses that grow too fast without these pillars in place often collapse under their own weight.

But those that take the time to strengthen their foundation stand the test of time, emerging as industry leaders rather than cautionary tales.

The Role of Patience in Building a Healthy and Ethical Business Culture

In a fast-moving economy like India's, patience is often overlooked in favor of quick wins and short-term profits. However, businesses that prioritize long-term sustainability over immediate gains are the ones that build lasting legacies. While some entrepreneurs have succeeded by bending the rules to their advantage, those who lay a foundation of ethical business practices create a culture of trust, stability, and resilience.

1. Ethical Growth vs. Shortcuts: The Long-Term Advantage

India's regulatory framework has evolved over time, but in the past, loopholes allowed businesses to manipulate policies for personal gain. Some industry giants thrived by influencing regulations to suit their needs. However, this path is not viable for most businesses. For entrepreneurs who lack the power to shape policies, the only reliable approach is to build a fundamentally strong and ethical business.

Though this takes longer, it significantly reduces the risk of failure. Businesses built on integrity and sound principles do not collapse overnight—they weather crises better, retain stakeholder trust, and grow sustainably.

2. The Personal Rewards of Ethical Leadership

Beyond financial success, ethical business practices contribute to peace of mind. Entrepreneurs who operate truthfully—paying their taxes, following regulations, and treating employees fairly—enjoy a clear conscience.

Consider the contrast: Many business leaders spend their nights worrying about the consequences of their shortcuts—unpaid dues, legal battles, and regulatory crackdowns. In contrast, those who build their companies with honesty sleep peacefully, free from the anxiety of looming repercussions.

3. Building an Organization Like a Family

A healthy business is not just about profits—it's about people. Entrepreneurs who invest in their employees, nurture a positive work environment, and lead with fairness create organizations that stand the test of time. A company that values its employees as much as its profit fosters loyalty, productivity, and innovation. The best businesses are not merely money-making machines; they are ecosystems that thrive because of the people who drive them.

4. Patience as a Strategic Asset

Patience allows businesses to develop strong foundations, make ethical decisions, and invest in their workforce. Rushing growth by cutting corners might yield temporary success, but it creates instability. Organizations that prioritize steady, principled growth not only last longer but also cultivate a culture of integrity and trust—essential ingredients for long-term prosperity.

The Power of Ethical, Patient Leadership

In a world where speed and profit often take precedence, patience remains an underrated yet crucial virtue in business. Entrepreneurs who focus on building people, fostering trust, and growing ethically create companies that endure. When business leaders treat their organizations with the same care and commitment as they would their own families, they set the foundation for success that spans generations. Patience in business is not just waiting; it's the strategic incubation of ideas.

3

Resisting the Rush

"The ability to manage expectations is the difference between success and disappointment."

— Tony Robbins

I remember the day I walked away from my stable, well-paying job. It wasn't a grand moment of celebration—it was terrifying. The comfort of a fixed salary, the structure of a routine, the security of knowing that at the end of the month, my expenses would be covered—all of that disappeared in an instant. What replaced it? An overwhelming sense of uncertainty and a gnawing anxiety kept me awake at night.

Stress Management During Early Days

I firmly believe that stress is an inevitable part of starting a new venture. When you transition from a stable, comfortable job into entrepreneurship, you leave behind financial security, structured routines, and a defined career path.

Most first-time entrepreneurs take this leap based on their ideas, confidence, and experience, but the reality of running a business is far more complex.

Limited finances, scarce resources, and a lack of industry connections make the journey even more challenging.

The stage of life at which you start your business also plays a crucial role. When I started mine, my son was only a year old. It was an incredibly trying time for my family. We lived in a rented apartment, and overnight, I went from having a reliable paycheck to relying entirely on my savings. Suddenly, every expense—rent, household necessities, and business costs—became my sole responsibility. The stress was overwhelming, and the constant pressure to succeed weighed heavily on me. I found myself repeatedly asking: *When will I start earning? When will success come?*

Every waking moment was consumed by thoughts of survival. Would I be able to sustain my family? Would I be able to pay my employees if I hired them? Would my business idea even work? These questions didn't just surface during the day—they followed me into the night, creeping into my thoughts when I should have been sleeping. I would often lie awake, running mental calculations, strategizing my next move, or simply drowning in self-doubt.

And yet, amid all that uncertainty, one thing was clear: there was no turning back. I had made my choice, and failure was not an option. I had to manage my stress, not let it manage me.

Navigating the Pressure

My biggest realization was that stress wasn't just an unfortunate side effect of starting a business—it was part of the package. And if I didn't learn to manage it, it would consume me.

So, I made a decision: I would not let stress dictate my life. I set strict work hours. Just because I was my own boss didn't mean I had to work myself into exhaustion. I made sure to take breaks, to step away from work in the evenings, to spend time with my family.

But discipline wasn't just about managing time. It was about managing my mind. I had to teach myself patience—something that doesn't come naturally when you're waiting for success. I reminded myself constantly: Rome wasn't built in a day. Businesses take time to grow. And more importantly, businesses built in a rush often collapse just as quickly. I also realized the importance of self-care. When you're an entrepreneur, your business is an extension of you. If you burn out, your business suffers. So, I made it a point to take care of my physical and mental well-being.

I exercised regularly, maintained a nutritious diet, and ensured I got enough sleep. It wasn't easy—there were days when stress threatened to take over, but I knew that if I didn't prioritize my health, I wouldn't be able to make rational business decisions.

Prioritizing Self-Care and Learning from Experience

One of the most valuable lessons I learned early on was the necessity of self-care. Entrepreneurship is demanding, and the pressure to succeed can drive you to push beyond your limits. But here's the harsh truth—burnout doesn't lead to success. It leads to exhaustion, poor decision-making, and ultimately, failure.

I saw it happen to peers—overworking themselves, sacrificing sleep, skipping meals, drowning in caffeine and alcohol to keep going. Some believed that working around the clock would bring them faster success. Instead, it drained them. Their energy, creativity, and ability to strategize suffered, and their businesses crumbled under the weight of their exhaustion.

I refused to let that happen to me. I embraced discipline—not just in my work but in my life. I stuck to a schedule, made time for exercise, ate balanced meals, and ensured I got enough rest. Even socializing had to be done in moderation. I had seen entrepreneurs fall into the trap of late-night networking, thinking it was essential for building connections. While relationships matter, I made it a point to keep my evenings free for family and personal downtime. After all, the stress of running a business doesn't just impact the entrepreneur—it affects their loved ones too.

Another crucial realization was that I didn't—and couldn't—know everything. When I started, I wasn't in a position of authority; I wasn't leading a team of hundreds. I was a frontline worker trying to establish myself. I lacked industry experience, and I knew that if I didn't seek guidance, I would struggle. I made it a habit to reach out to others who had walked the same path. Some had left their jobs to start their own businesses, just like I had. We shared experiences, exchanged advice, and learned from one another. There's no shame in asking for help—if anything, it's a necessity. I also sought mentorship from seasoned professionals. Some were retired executives, and others were experienced entrepreneurs who had seen the ups and downs of business.

Their insights were invaluable. Learning from their experiences helped me navigate the early challenges of my journey with more confidence and clarity.

The Reality of Entrepreneurship

The truth is, you are never fully prepared for the stress that comes with being an entrepreneur. You can anticipate financial difficulties, you can plan for slow months, but the emotional weight of it all is something you can only experience firsthand.

There were moments when I questioned everything. When things didn't go according to plan, when progress was slower than I had hoped, when doubts from others began creeping into my own mind. Society has a way of glamorizing entrepreneurship, making it seem like an exhilarating journey filled with big wins and groundbreaking moments. But in reality, it is a test of patience, resilience, and sheer determination.

What got me through those early days was clarity. Clarity in my purpose, in my goals, and in my belief that patience and perseverance would eventually pay off. The stress never fully goes away, but with time, you learn to manage it. You learn that success isn't a finish line you sprint towards—it's a journey you walk, step by step, with patience and resilience.

And so, I kept moving forward.

Scaling up and its Challenges

As a business grows, particularly when you're scaling from 100 to 200 employees, the journey can feel like a rollercoaster. It usually takes about five to seven years if you're moving in the right direction, but with that growth comes a new set of challenges—ones you never anticipated. You start facing things like managing complex factory operations and dealing with unions, and that's when the pressure really builds. And let me tell you—navigating these hurdles requires more than just sharp business acumen. It demands immense patience, calm under fire, and unwavering leadership.

In my own experience, I've found that the first five to six years are crucial in laying the groundwork for strong management practices, whether you're dealing with your sales team or operations on the factory floor. When I first took on a single factory, I didn't just oversee operations from behind a desk.

I spent time—real, meaningful time—on the shop floor every day. At least an hour, sometimes more, just walking around, talking to workers, understanding their challenges, and watching how they worked.

I knew every single worker by name, and I made it a point to engage with them personally—whether it was asking about their day or checking in on their tasks.

This wasn't just about creating a friendly work environment; it was about building trust—trust that would hold when times get tough. And trust me, times did get tough. When you're working in a factory, where stress levels can run high and the stakes are always high, maintaining that trust is everything. Those small, consistent interactions formed the foundation for preventing labor unrest and for keeping the company grounded during difficult times.

Now, as the company grew, it became impossible to maintain that level of personal engagement with every worker. But the culture I instilled remained—it had to. That culture of direct, personal engagement became the lifeblood of our operations. The philosophy of treating every employee as an individual, of truly caring about their well-being, is what laid the foundation for a cohesive and resilient workforce. It became the backbone of everything we did, and without it, I don't think we could have navigated the challenges that came with growth.

Another challenge that comes with growth is visibility. Once your revenue reaches ₹80-100 crore, your business stops being just a local player—you start drawing attention from all directions. Suddenly, it's not just about keeping your industry peers at bay. Now, you're on the radar of politicians, bureaucrats, and other influential figures. This attention isn't always welcome, and handling it requires finesse.

The moment people see you succeeding, they want a piece of that success. When you drive a better car or live in a bigger house, you don't just get admiration—you get targets. Politicians often expect favors, and in India, that can mean anything from supporting their events to making financial contributions. The whole system of political funding here is much murkier than in countries like the US, where business donations are legally structured and transparent. In India, the more successful you become, the more you're pulled into this web of political expectations. It's a delicate dance—becoming a successful entrepreneur can quickly turn you into a target for political and bureaucratic interests.

Over time, I've learned the hard way that the best strategy is to stay neutral. Staying neutral might sound simple, but it's actually one of the most challenging aspects of being in business.

Aligning with any political party can be disastrous—every election cycle brings in new leaders, and every party has its own allies and enemies. If you back one party, you automatically make yourself a target for their rivals once the political tide changes.

That's why I've chosen to remain polite and cordial but non-committal. I don't engage in political favoritism, but I also don't completely cut off these interactions. You can't avoid them. But you have to navigate them wisely, balancing your business needs with the political currents around you. It's a skill that takes years to master, but if you want to protect your company's interests, it's absolutely essential. When you have a strong relationship with your employees, they don't just see you as their boss—they see you as someone who genuinely cares about their well-being. That kind of trust goes a long way, especially when you hit a rough patch. I've seen this firsthand.

There was one particular moment that stood out. One of our employees was going through a personal crisis—a family situation that was weighing heavily on him. His work started slipping, and his performance was affected. Now, most managers might have overlooked it or simply viewed it as a performance issue. But because I had built a relationship with him over time, I knew something was wrong. I wasn't just looking at his numbers or his output—I was looking at *him*. And I could tell he wasn't his usual self.

I reached out to him directly—no formalities, just a personal conversation. He opened up to me about what was going on, and I made sure to offer him support, not just as an employee but as a person. We helped lighten his workload for a while and gave him the time he needed to deal with his situation.

What followed was remarkable. Not only did his performance improve once his personal situation stabilized, but his loyalty to the company grew tenfold. That level of engagement—that personal touch—wasn't just about solving a work issue. It was about creating a sense of belonging and trust that runs deeper than anything purely professional. When employees feel like their company cares about them beyond just the numbers, that's when you start building a truly invested workforce.

The Evolution of Workplace Culture: From Close-Knit to Scalable Trust

In the early days of a company, direct engagement with employees is easy. You walk the factory floor, have conversations, and personally resolve issues. But as an organization grows, it becomes impossible to maintain that level of interaction. That's when culture takes over. A well-established company culture ensures that trust, respect, and integrity remain intact, even when leadership is physically distant.

I've seen this dynamic play out time and again, especially in moments of crisis.

Crisis and Compassion: Lessons from the COVID-19 Pandemic

The COVID-19 pandemic was a defining moment for businesses worldwide. For us, it was a test of leadership and our commitment to our employees. We lost a few employees to the virus—a tragedy that shook the entire workforce. In such moments, employees don't just look for financial compensation; they seek reassurance, empathy, and solidarity. They want to know that their company stands with them.

But the reality was stark—revenues were down, cash flow was tight, and even basic operations were under strain. Paying salaries on time was already a challenge, yet we knew we had to act.

Rather than making a top-down, unilateral decision, we formed a committee with HR, senior managers, and the colleagues of the deceased employees. We tasked them with coming up with a fair recommendation. The key here was restraint—I consciously chose not to influence their decision, knowing that people are more likely to accept an outcome they helped shape. The committee consulted with the bereaved families and insurance providers. I expected them to propose ₹10 lakh in additional support, but they recommended ₹5 lakh. Without hesitation, we decided to go a step further and offered ₹7 lakh. This wasn't just about money—it was about showing our people that we valued them beyond their work. It reinforced trust, goodwill, and our core values in a way no policy or speech ever could.

The Unthinkable Tragedy: Leadership in the Face of Loss

Some decisions test your leadership at the deepest level.

Recently, a long-serving worker, who had dedicated his life to our company, was set to retire at 58. He was in good health, eager to continue working, and had requested an extension, which we generally allow at a fixed salary. Then, the unimaginable happened.

One day, while on duty, he slipped and fell into a vat of boiling water. The accident was swift and horrifying. He was pulled out immediately and rushed to a private hospital. For a time, it seemed like he would recover, but due to complications—perhaps from shock or internal injuries—he passed away.

In such situations, panic and chaos can easily take over. The legal process alone is overwhelming—mandatory reports to the SDM, labor department investigations, safety audits, and worst of all, the rampant bureaucracy that often forces businesses to pay bribes just to clear paperwork.

But we took a different approach.

Once again, we formed a committee, this time with HR, factory management, and representatives from the workers' families. The discussions led to two key requests: first, the worker's son, who was struggling in an unsatisfactory job elsewhere, asked for employment in the company. We immediately agreed—this was the least we could do for a family that had lost its provider. Second, the committee recommended an ex gratia payment of ₹10 lakh, in addition to the insurance payout. We accepted this without hesitation.

This wasn't just about following a process—it was about honoring a life, ensuring a family's stability, and maintaining the dignity of our workforce. By handling the situation with empathy, transparency, and mutual agreement, we avoided unnecessary disputes, legal complications, and most importantly, any resentment among our employees. At the end of the day, leadership isn't about dictating terms—it's about building trust. A well-run company isn't just measured by its profits, but by how it handles adversity, how it treats its people, and how it upholds its values even when times are tough.

These stories aren't just incidents; they're proof that a business built on respect, fairness, and integrity will always endure.

Employees don't forget how they were treated in difficult times. And in the long run, goodwill is the most valuable currency any company can have.

The Psychological Impact of Societal Pressure and Setting Realistic Milestones

Success in business is often measured in numbers like revenue, market share, and growth percentages. But behind those numbers lie people—employees, managers, and leaders—who bear the weight of achieving them. And too often, the pressure to succeed, especially in a society that glorifies rapid growth, becomes an invisible burden that leads to stress, attrition, and ultimately, failure.

The Trap of Unrealistic Expectations

One of the most common mistakes businesses make is setting targets that are simply unattainable. Management, in its eagerness to drive performance, often imposes growth figures that look impressive on paper but are detached from reality. The result? Employees feel the weight of expectations they cannot meet. Incentives become elusive, morale plummets, and soon, the best talent starts looking for opportunities elsewhere.

I've seen this happen time and again. A company sets a target based on ambition rather than capability. Sales teams, eager to prove themselves, push beyond reasonable limits, only to fall short.

Frustration builds, incentives remain out of reach, and stress replaces motivation. Eventually, the cycle of unrealistic goals and unmet expectations leads to high attrition rates, which further disrupts stability.

A Balanced Approach to Growth

The key to sustainable success is balance—ambition tempered with realism. When setting targets, we first analyze industry benchmarks. Every sector has a natural growth rate, and understanding where our company fits within that framework is crucial. If the industry is growing at 10%, we evaluate our own resources, strengths, and past performance. Maybe we have the capacity to achieve 8%, maybe 7%. We don't set goals arbitrarily; we set them through honest discussion.

Of course, as entrepreneurs, we want the highest possible growth. But setting a target that employees believe in is more powerful than chasing an unattainable number. If they say 7% is realistic, we might push for 8%—just enough to challenge them, but not enough to overwhelm them. Growth is still growth.

The Power of Achievable Targets

A well-set target is not just a number—it's a psychological motivator. When employees see that their goals are within reach, their confidence increases. They work with purpose, knowing that their efforts will be rewarded. Stress levels decrease, productivity improves, and the entire organization functions more efficiently.

More importantly, when employees achieve realistic milestones, they feel a sense of ownership in the company's success. Their performance is recognized, their incentives are attainable, and they see themselves as integral to the company's future. The employer-employee relationship shifts from one of pressure to one of collaboration.

By setting realistic milestones, businesses foster an environment where employees can thrive rather than survive. Growth becomes a steady climb rather than a desperate sprint.

And in the long run, companies that prioritize sustainable success over short-term wins stand the test of time. The pressure to achieve rapid success in business is relentless. Investors, stakeholders, and even competitors push a narrative that growth must be exponential, immediate, and overwhelming. But the truth is, sustainable businesses are built on measured, consistent progress—not reckless ambition.

The Weight of Societal Expectations

When I first ventured into entrepreneurship, I quickly realized that societal pressure comes in many forms. It's not just about financial expectations; it's about external demands that can make an already difficult journey even more challenging. Communities, regulators, and even employees have expectations that, at times, seem impossible to meet in the early days of a business.

Take, for example, the challenge of setting up a pharmaceutical manufacturing unit. In the initial phases, we had limited resources. We rented factory space and focused on production, but we couldn't afford an expensive water treatment system immediately. Meanwhile, the local community saw colored waste being discharged and assumed we were recklessly polluting their environment. They didn't see our financial constraints or the steps we were taking to improve the situation—they only saw a problem that needed fixing.

This is where societal pressure becomes a double-edged sword.

On the one hand, these concerns are valid, and as responsible entrepreneurs, we must address them. On the other hand, an early-stage business cannot solve every issue overnight. The expectation that an entrepreneur should instantly comply with every norm, provide jobs for the local community, and minimize operational disruptions while barely keeping their business afloat is overwhelming.

Instead of taking an adversarial approach, we prioritized relationship-building. We engaged with the local community, explained our situation, apologized for any inconvenience, and assured them that we were actively working toward a solution. By maintaining transparency and open communication, we managed to turn resistance into cooperation.

A similar challenge arose with hiring expectations. The local community expected us to employ their people, even when the required skill set wasn't available. As a pharmaceutical business, we needed trained professionals, and unfortunately, not everyone in the community had the necessary expertise. However, instead of outright rejecting these expectations, we created a middle ground—we provided skill training programs to help interested candidates meet the qualifications required for employment. This approach allowed us to balance both business needs and community expectations without compromising on operational efficiency.

Business growth should be a steady climb, not a desperate sprint. When entrepreneurs give in to societal and investor pressure to scale too quickly, they often overextend their resources, make hasty decisions, and ultimately burn out. The most successful companies are those that prioritize long-term sustainability over short-term wins. The lesson here is clear: push for growth, but never at the expense of your people, your employees, or your integrity. A business flourishes when it is built on a foundation of trust—when employees feel supported rather than overburdened, when goals are ambitious yet achievable, and when success is measured not just in financial gains, but in long-term impact. Sustainable success is not about how fast you can grow—it's about how well you build. Businesses that prioritize thoughtful decision-making, adaptability, and responsible growth will outlast those that chase short-term victories.

The pressure to scale rapidly will always exist, but true leadership lies in knowing when to push forward and when to pace yourself.

Because in the end, the companies that endure are the ones that grow with purpose, resilience, and a vision beyond immediate gains.

A disciplined and well-structured life is not just beneficial for personal well-being but also crucial for long-term business success. Waking up refreshed with a clear mind is far more effective than struggling through the day after late-night indulgences. The way you manage yourself reflects on your business, and ultimately, people follow the example you set. When you cultivate balance and discipline, you inspire those around you to do the same, creating a healthier and more productive work culture.

1. Patience is essential. Managing stress and expectations requires a long-term mindset, leading to more thoughtful and strategic business decisions.

2. Mental and physical well-being impact business success. A business thrives when its leader is in good health—mentally, physically, and emotionally.

3. Success is a product of well-managed stress and realistic expectations. Rushing toward quick wins can lead to poor decisions and burnout.

4. Discipline fosters clarity and productivity. Maintaining a balanced lifestyle, setting boundaries on work hours, and avoiding unhealthy habits create a more sustainable entrepreneurial journey.

5. Leadership is about setting an example. Employees and peers often look up to you, and the habits you cultivate—whether structured work schedules, prioritizing rest, or managing stress effectively—can inspire and influence your organization's culture.

Entrepreneurship is not just about financial gains—it is about sustainability, resilience, and building something that lasts. The strongest businesses are those built on patience, strategic decision-making, and a mindset that prioritizes long-term stability over fleeting success.

And so, I kept walking.

4

The Honest Enterprise

Building a Culture of Trust

*"Honesty and transparency make you vulnerable.
Be honest and transparent anyway."*
— Mother Teresa

A *single grain of sand in the cogwheel can halt the mightiest of machines.* In the intricate mechanics of a business, honesty is not just a moral choice; it is the very oil that keeps the gears turning smoothly. More than an ethical principle, honesty is the foundation on which lasting enterprises are built, shaping brand identity, internal culture, and external relationships.

The Pillar of Truth: Honesty as the Cornerstone of Business Integrity

When I started my journey as an entrepreneur, I realized one thing very early on—honesty isn't just a moral choice; it's the bedrock of a thriving business.

Without it, an organization, no matter how grand, is like a house of cards waiting to collapse.

I have seen businesses rise and fall, and the common denominator in their downfall has often been a lack of integrity. Honesty is not just a corporate value you hang on the wall—it has to be lived, breathed, and reflected in every decision, every interaction, every deal.

As a leader, your actions are always under a microscope. People watch, they observe, and—whether consciously or unconsciously—they emulate. If you lead with honesty, your team will follow suit. But if you resort to manipulation or deceit, that too will trickle down into the company culture. In many organizations, I've seen how dishonesty at the top—whether it's tweaking financial reports or making under-the-table deals—quickly seeps into every level. Employees start cutting corners, customers lose trust, and the brand's credibility begins to erode. The tone you set is the culture you build. The choice is simple but profound. I've seen companies where dishonesty starts small—a little tweak in the accounts, an under-the-table deal to get things done faster. These small infractions soon become a way of life, shaping a culture where employees assume that bending the truth is just "how business works." Before long, such companies find themselves entangled in reputational damage, legal troubles, and worst of all, a complete erosion of trust.

On the other hand, let's take an example that inspires us all—the Tata Group. When you hear the name Tata, what comes to mind? *Trust. Integrity. Transparency.* For decades, Tata has built not just a business, but a legacy of honesty. Their commitment to ethical business practices is so ingrained in their DNA that they have never been associated with corruption or deceit. That kind of trust isn't built overnight; it's earned, consistently, over years of doing the right thing—even when no one is watching.

In my own business, honesty has been our guiding light. We deal with distributors, stockists, and countless stakeholders, and disagreements are inevitable. However, what has always helped us is that people know that when an issue reaches management, it will be resolved fairly, without favoritism or hidden agendas. This reputation didn't come easy, but it has become our most valuable asset. It eliminates unnecessary conflicts, ensures long-term loyalty, and builds an unshakable foundation of trust.

Honesty doesn't just build trust—it enhances reputation. A company known for integrity gains goodwill that no marketing budget can buy. More than that, honesty offers a strategic advantage.

It ensures sustainability in an era where corporate scandals frequently make headlines. Customers today are more discerning than ever; they value authenticity. Investors seek companies that operate with transparency. Employees want to work in environments where ethics aren't just spoken about but practiced.

So, as business leaders, we must ask ourselves—are we building organizations that will stand the test of time? Are we setting the right example for those who follow in our footsteps? The answer lies in the choices we make every day. The path of honesty may not always be the easiest, but it is, without a doubt, the one that leads to enduring success.

Honesty in business goes beyond merely avoiding lies—it is about fostering transparency, reliability, and ethical decision-making at every level. It dictates how businesses operate, how leaders lead, and how employees interact.

More importantly, it determines how customers, investors, and stakeholders perceive an organization.

Lessons from Ethical Business Practices

A strong reputation is the bedrock of any successful business. It's not just about selling a product or service; it's about establishing trust, ensuring transparency, and showing integrity in every aspect of what you do. Whether you are in pharmaceuticals like us or any other industry, customers and clients seek reliability, honesty, and consistency. They want to know that the company they're dealing with operates with integrity and a sense of responsibility.

At Psychotropics India Limited (PIL), we have cultivated that kind of trust. Our customers—doctors, hospitals, and healthcare institutions—are not only our clients, but partners in building a healthier world. And we didn't get here by cutting corners. No, we got here by ensuring that the systems we use, the processes we follow, and the products we deliver are of the highest quality, manufactured with utmost honesty and transparency. It's why even the top hospitals in the region are willing to pay a little more for our products. They know they can trust us to deliver exactly what we promise.

In the pharmaceutical industry, trust is everything. And trust is rooted in honesty and integrity. When these values guide every decision, whether big or small, it ensures that the business not only survives but thrives. Ethical decision-making becomes second nature. There's no room for anything less than doing the right thing.

This creates an organizational culture where ethics aren't just buzzwords; they are part of the company's DNA. A company's core values shape its behavior, guide decision-making, and set the foundation for long-term success. When honesty is deeply embedded in the DNA of a business, it fosters a culture where trust is not only encouraged but expected.

What's more, fostering a culture of honesty leads to accountability. At PIL, no one fears admitting mistakes.

If something goes wrong, we don't shy away from owning up to it. We've created an environment where accountability is not met with punishment but with constructive solutions. Everyone is encouraged to speak openly, and it only strengthens the business. The end result is a transparent and ethical organization that not only follows the rules but also sets new standards for others to follow.

If I had to sum it up in a single takeaway, it would be this: *honesty is the foundation on which an ethical organization is built.* When trust, transparency, and ethical behavior are core values for your employees, your customers, and your stakeholders, everything else falls into place.

I couldn't think of a better example to illustrate this than the Tata Group. Their commitment to ethical business practices has helped them build an enduring reputation, not just in India but around the world. The Tatas' integrity has opened doors to numerous other partnerships. Take Tata Motors, for example. From building trucks and cars to now venturing into electric vehicles, Tata has shown that their reputation for quality and trust is consistent across all sectors. And then there's Tata Steel, a leading player in the raw materials market, and Tata Consultancy Services, one of the world's largest IT services companies. Even in healthcare, they've built one of the largest cancer hospitals in Mumbai. What's remarkable about all of these businesses is that they are driven by the same core principles of honesty, transparency, and dedication to doing what's best for everyone involved.

And let's not forget about Tata's acquisition of Jaguar. They didn't just buy a company; they integrated it into their ecosystem with the same values they apply across all their businesses. Though Jaguar's operations were based in the UK, Tata moved the manufacturing to India to lower costs, but not at the expense of the workforce.

They handled the shift with diligence, ensuring that the local employees were treated fairly, in full accordance with local laws.

This level of care and consideration only further cements Tata's reputation as a business that acts with integrity.

The success of any organization comes down to one thing: the strength of its reputation. A business built on honesty, transparency, and ethical decision-making doesn't just attract customers—it fosters long-lasting relationships, attracts partnerships, and creates a legacy that stands the test of time. At Psychotropics India Limited, we strive to follow that same path, ensuring that our values are at the core of everything we do. This is the way forward for any business that truly wants to make a difference.

A company known for its honesty creates a competitive advantage. Customers are willing to pay a premium for brands they trust, and employees are more likely to stay with organizations that value integrity.

The Ripple Effect: How Honesty Impacts Internal and External Relationships

Honesty within a business impacts two key groups: the internal team and external stakeholders.

Internal Team Dynamics: A culture of honesty fosters accountability, reduces fear, and promotes ethical decision-making. Employees who know they can admit mistakes without fear of retribution are more likely to innovate and take ownership of their work. When mistakes are acknowledged openly, solutions can be found faster, and trust between teams strengthens.

In our organization, if an employee makes an error, we don't hide it—we fix it. If you know the company will support you for being honest, you don't waste time covering up mistakes.

That speeds up efficiency, builds trust, and ultimately strengthens the company.

External Business Relationships: Trust in business relationships is currency. Distributors, vendors, and investors want to work with companies that operate transparently.

Consider the pharmaceutical industry, where compliance and transparency are critical. Hospitals and medical professionals rely on drug manufacturers who operate with integrity. A company that ensures accurate reporting, follows ethical guidelines, and refrains from manipulating data will always find itself in a stronger position than one that cuts corners.

At PIL, transparency isn't just something we talk about—it's something we actively implement in every corner of our business.

We're a small company, but we believe in setting high standards, and our commitment to ethical practices is at the core of everything we do. One of the key ways we've built transparency into our operations is by ensuring that senior management and our team are always on the same page. When a senior manager has a decision to make, they approach me with their thoughts and ideas. We've worked together long enough that I can trust their judgment, and they know I'll support them as long as it aligns with our values and the way we work. There's no gap in understanding between management and employees, and that alignment has been crucial to our success.

This shared philosophy is especially important because of the scale of our operations. With multiple factories and close to 1,600 employees, communication can easily become fragmented. Without a unified approach, things can get messy. Imagine trying to run a business by sending a WhatsApp message here and an email there. It quickly becomes a game of Chinese whispers, and that's when things start to fall apart.

Without transparency, you won't have clarity—and without clarity, you won't have a strong, ethical business.

To ensure we stay on track, we've focused on building a consistent company culture where everyone is familiar with the principles we stand for. No matter how large our team gets, everyone knows what's expected and how we operate. This alignment ensures that we can move forward with confidence, knowing that decisions are made based on the same set of values. So, whether we're dealing with day-to-day operations or strategic decisions, transparency is woven into everything we do. We've learned that a clear, ethical approach to decision-making is the best way to keep the business running smoothly, even as it grows. In the end, transparency isn't just a value we uphold—it's the reason we've built such a strong and reliable organization.

Transparency as a Crisis Management Strategy

In times of crisis, transparency becomes an invaluable asset. When businesses attempt to cover up problems—be it financial difficulties, product recalls, or service failures—the backlash is often far worse than the crisis itself. A prime example is the Tylenol poisoning crisis faced by Johnson & Johnson in 1982. Instead of downplaying the issue, the company immediately issued public warnings, recalled products, and cooperated fully with authorities. Their honesty saved lives and, in the long run, reinforced trust in the brand. Compare this to cases where companies have concealed product defects or financial mismanagement, resulting in irreversible reputational damage.

The Long-Term Damage of Dishonesty

History is littered with cautionary tales of companies that collapsed due to dishonest practices. Enron, Volkswagen's emissions scandal, and the fall of Theranos serve as stark reminders of the consequences of deception. While dishonesty might bring short-term gains, it inevitably leads to long-term fallout.

Rebuilding a Brand Through Honesty: The Domino's Pizza Transformation

One of the most compelling examples of a company that turned its reputation around through sheer honesty is Domino's Pizza. By the late 2000s, the brand had hit rock bottom—customers were vocal about their dissatisfaction, criticizing everything from the taste of the pizza to the quality of ingredients. Social media was flooded with negative reviews, and consumer surveys ranked Domino's as one of the worst-tasting pizza chains in the U.S.

For many companies, the typical response to such criticism would have been damage control—perhaps tweaking the recipe slightly, rolling out a new marketing campaign, or simply ignoring the complaints, hoping they would die down. But Domino's took a different, far more radical approach: they faced the criticism head-on.

Instead of brushing aside the complaints, Domino's launched an unprecedentedly honest advertising campaign called *"The Pizza Turnaround"* in 2009. In a series of commercials and digital content, they openly admitted that their pizza wasn't good enough. They aired real, unfiltered customer feedback—harsh reviews that most brands would have buried.

Some of the criticism included statements like:

- *"Domino's crust tastes like cardboard."*
- *"The sauce is bland and tastes like ketchup."*
- *"This is the worst excuse for a pizza I've ever had."*

The brand didn't just acknowledge the backlash; they put their own product under the microscope and validated the complaints.

Their CEO at the time, Patrick Doyle, appeared in commercials stating, *"We heard you. We listened. And we're changing."*

Owning up to flaws was only the first step. Dominos didn't stop at admissions—they completely revamped their recipe. They changed everything:

- A new sauce with a bolder flavor;
- A better crust that wasn't just an afterthought
- Higher quality cheese for improved taste and texture

They documented the entire process in behind-the-scenes videos, showing real chefs and food experts working on the improvements. They even invited some of their biggest critics to try the new recipe on camera, capturing their reactions as they realized the pizza had genuinely improved.

The Results: A Game-Changing Comeback

The gamble paid off. The honesty-driven campaign sparked a massive wave of consumer goodwill. Customers appreciated the transparency, and even those who had sworn off Domino's gave the new recipe a try. The brand saw a 14.3% increase in same-store sales in Q1 of 2010, the largest quarterly sales jump in company history.

Beyond the numbers, Domino's earned back customer trust—a commodity far more valuable than any short-term revenue spike. Their transformation became a case study in corporate authenticity, proving that admitting mistakes and committing to real change could breathe new life into a struggling brand.

The Takeaway: They admitted their pizza needed improvement, took customer feedback seriously, and made changes accordingly. The result? A complete brand turnaround and a significant boost in customer trust. Domino's didn't just improve its pizza; they redefined how businesses should handle criticism.

Instead of hiding flaws, they leaned into them, embraced transparency, and turned a weakness into a strength. Today, the brand is stronger than ever, expanding its global reach and consistently innovating in the fast-food space.

This case underscores that honesty isn't just about ethics—it's a powerful business differentiator. When used correctly, it can rebuild reputations, regain customer trust, and ultimately, drive success.

Our Business Truths: Integrity Over Shortcuts

In any business, there are moments that test your commitment to your values—moments where the easy path seems tempting, but the right path requires difficult decisions. I recall an incident early on when we were dealing with a product filing process that required submitting detailed documentation. One of the key conditions was that we had to prove that we had been manufacturing the product for a certain number of years—let's say five or seven, depending on the case.

In the pharmaceutical industry, especially, accurate documentation and paperwork are everything. Every product we manufacture, every approval we seek, and every regulation we adhere to is built on a foundation of documentation. It's a process where integrity is constantly tested, and the temptation to take shortcuts is real.

It's a tricky situation because sometimes, especially when a product is new, the data or documentation to prove these conditions simply doesn't exist. That's when the temptation to take shortcuts creeps in. It's not uncommon for businesses to either fabricate the data or avoid answering difficult questions. After all, a product that doesn't meet certain criteria might mean losing out on a significant business opportunity.

One of my institutional managers came to me with exactly that kind of situation. I remember a conversation with him that truly reinforced what we stood for as a company.

"Sir, there's a huge opportunity here," he said, presenting a product registration file. "The competition is minimal—just one other company. If we can just adjust the documents a little, tweak the details to meet the eligibility criteria, we can secure this business. It's just paperwork."

I leaned back, taking in his words. The logic was tempting. The numbers made sense. But the ethics? That was non-negotiable.

"If we're eligible, we go for it," I said firmly. "If not, we don't file. Simple as that."

"But sir, the business potential—"

He suggested that maybe we could "prepare" the missing data or find a way around the condition. Essentially, he was asking, "Why not bend the rules just this once to get the deal?" But we didn't, and we never would. I made it clear that if we weren't eligible for the product, we simply wouldn't file the documents.

If we couldn't meet the conditions, then it was a no-go.

"I don't care how big the opportunity is. If we're not eligible, we don't fake it. That's not who we are."

It wasn't the first time I had encountered this kind of suggestion, and I knew it wouldn't be the last. The industry is full of grey areas, and many justify small manipulations in the name of competitive advantage. But for us, the principle was clear—we would never compromise our honesty for profit.

There have been situations when I had to explain this multiple times, but the message was always the same: "We don't compromise on our integrity, no matter what."

As tempting as that business opportunity was, I knew that going down that path would only lead to regret. We've always operated with the belief that we must be able to sleep peacefully at night—without any lingering guilt. That's why, even though we were a small company, we made the conscious decision to follow the same principles as some of the best organizations out there, like the Tata conglomerate. Honesty and integrity were non-negotiable for us.

We chose honesty. We walked away from that deal. It wasn't easy, but the long-term benefits far outweighed the short-term gains. That single decision reinforced our company's reputation, and years later, the same client returned—because they knew we were the kind of business that valued integrity over profits.

This philosophy extends to every part of our operations. We've also made it a point never to pay bribes, never push papers under the table, and never seek shortcuts to speed up approvals. Sure, it has meant waiting two or sometimes three months for decisions that others might get in weeks. There were instances when decisions took way longer than expected, but we never gave in.

The result? Over time, people came to trust us because they knew we wouldn't cut corners. Our reputation grew, and it wasn't just about the business we did; it was about how we did it.

We dealt with people on the basis of integrity, and they dealt with us the same way. And that's a reputation you can only build over time, one that becomes the backbone of your company. It wasn't just about the sale or the contract—it was about creating a company that people could trust. And for us, that's worth far more than any short-term gain.

Today, when people deal with us, they know exactly who and what they're working with.

No underhanded dealings, no hidden clauses, no backroom negotiations—just business done the right way. And that's a reputation worth far more than any single deal.

Because at the end of the day, *a business isn't just about profits— it's about knowing you've built something that stands on integrity.*

So how can businesses actively foster honesty and transparency in their operations?

1. Establish Clear Ethical Guidelines: Make integrity a non-negotiable part of company culture. Document ethical guidelines and communicate them regularly to employees.

2. Encourage Open Communication: Employees should feel safe to voice concerns without fear of retaliation. Anonymous reporting channels can help expose unethical practices early.

3. Be Honest in Marketing and Sales: Exaggerated claims or misleading advertising may boost short-term sales but can destroy credibility in the long run. Always deliver on promises.

4. Lead by Example: Executives and managers must embody the honesty they expect from employees. When leadership demonstrates transparency, it sets the standard for the entire organization.

5. Regular Audits and Accountability Measures: Third-party audits, clear documentation, and compliance checks ensure that ethical practices are being followed consistently.

Key Takeaways

- A culture of honesty is a business's greatest asset in building lasting relationships.
- Transparency leads to accountability, which fosters a strong, positive workplace.
- Trust is not just an ethical bonus—it's a competitive edge.

Identify an area in your business where greater transparency could be implemented. Take one step towards that transparency and observe the reactions from stakeholders.

As we affirm the power of honesty in unlocking business potential, we prepare to tackle the delicate balance of ethics in the competitive arena. In the next chapter, we explore how ethical behavior withstands the test of time and paves a golden path for those who walk it.

5

Ethics in Business

"Ethics is knowing the difference between what you have a right to do and what is right to do."

— Potter Stewart

In the fast-paced and competitive business world, companies are often faced with choices that test their ethical foundations. While some may prioritize short-term financial gains, those who embrace ethical decision-making find themselves reaping long-term benefits that far outweigh any temporary profits. Ethical behavior is not just a moral choice—it is a strategic advantage that enhances brand reputation, builds stakeholder trust, and ensures business sustainability.

A company built on ethical values isn't just following a roadmap—it is creating a legacy of trust, stability, and long-term success. This is not a quick fix or a short-term maneuver; it is a commitment to integrity that defines how a business operates, how it treats its people, and how it engages with the world. When a company stands firm in its ethical approach, it builds an unshakable foundation—one that stands the test of time and outlasts market fluctuations, economic downturns, and changing business landscapes. The most trusted businesses today, the ones that have endured for decades and even centuries, didn't rely on fleeting trends or short-term tactics.

Instead, they cultivated a culture of ethics and honesty, making decisions that aligned with their core values. Take Biocon Ltd. as an example. Founded by Kiran Mazumdar-Shaw in 1978, the business has grown from a small enzyme company into a global biopharmaceutical leader. What sets Biocon apart is its commitment to affordable innovation, making life-saving drugs like insulin and cancer treatments accessible to underprivileged communities. The company prioritizes quality, transparency, and social impact while striking a balance between scientific excellence and strong ethical values. Even during the COVID-19 crisis, Biocon provided cost-effective solutions to public health initiatives. The company has built long-term trust and a global reputation by prioritizing purpose over profit.

It is not merely about doing the right thing; it is about forging a foundation so strong that no storm can shake it. Looking back, I see how this principle shaped my journey, how it transformed my business from a fledgling venture into a formidable force in the industry. The rewards of integrity may not always be immediate, but they are enduring. The strategic advantage of this approach became evident over time. Ethical companies build trust—not just with customers but with employees, stakeholders, investors, and even financial institutions. When people believe in your credibility, they rally behind you. Amul, for instance, is more than just a dairy brand—it's a movement built on trust and farmer empowerment. Customers have remained loyal to them for life because of their dependability and ethical practices.

I have witnessed this firsthand in my own company. My first employee, who joined when we were operating on a shoestring budget, still works with us today. He rose through the ranks and now holds a senior position as VP in the organization. That level of loyalty, that kind of dedication, is only possible when employees know they are working for a company that operates with integrity. People don't just work for a paycheck; they stay when they believe in the company's values. His journey is not just a personal success story but a testament to the strength of ethical leadership. People stay where they feel valued, where they believe in the mission, and where they know their hard work contributes to something meaningful.

High employee retention is not just about financial incentives; it is about the culture of trust and integrity that a company fosters.

Ethics cannot be a mere strategy; it must come from within, be ingrained in the organization's DNA. It is the foundation of any enduring business and the best practice across industries. Companies built on ethical principles do not just survive market fluctuations—they thrive over generations, earning trust that translates into lasting success. Consider the Godrej Group, an iconic Indian conglomerate that is a testament to ethical business practices. What started as a humble lock-making enterprise in 1897 gradually expanded into steel almirahs—an essential fixture in Indian households. Over the years, Godrej diversified into consumer goods, cosmetics, and real estate, yet one thing remained constant—its commitment to trust and integrity. Today, whenever Godrej launches a new real estate project, it sells out within days. That is not just a reflection of demand; it is a demonstration of decades of credibility. Customers, investors, and stakeholders know that a Godrej project means quality, reliability, and transparency. Such a reputation is not built overnight—it is earned through generations of ethical business practices.

The same holds true for Hindustan Unilever Limited (HUL). Founded in 1933, the company built its empire on consumer trust. It is another prime example of unwavering integrity. HUL has been a household name in India for nearly a century. From food products and personal care to household cleaning solutions, the company has meticulously built trust across diverse sectors. One of their earliest and most successful products, Dalda, became synonymous with *vanaspati ghee* to the extent that consumers did not ask for a brand—they asked for "Dalda." This was not just the result of aggressive marketing but of product reliability and ethical business practices. Ethical companies do not just sell products; they forge enduring relationships with their consumers, creating loyalty that spans generations.

The lesson here is clear—ethical businesses endure. Companies that chase short-term gains through dubious means often disappear just as quickly as they rise. The market is littered with examples of businesses that soared through unethical shortcuts only to crumble under the weight of their own misdeeds. Corruption may offer instant gratification, but it is a ticking time bomb. Ethical decision-making, on the other hand, builds a strong, stable foundation that withstands market volatility, regulatory scrutiny, and shifts in consumer behavior.

Consider Fevicol as an example. Over the decades, it has become a household name and a symbol of unbreakable trust, both literally and figuratively. Fevicol, which is produced by Pidilite Industries, is more than simply a product; it is a well-known brand that has gained the trust of consumers, contractors, and carpenters alike. Whether it's professional-grade adhesives or DIY solutions, Fevicol stands for reliability, quality, and consistency. Its iconic advertising and customer-first strategy have fostered a bond with the Indian public that extends far beyond marketing.

Fevicol's enduring market trust is a result of decades of product performance, ethical business conduct, and a lifelong commitment to quality.

Beyond trust and reputation, ethical businesses also enjoy financial resilience. Investors, lenders, and financial institutions prefer companies with clean records. Ethical companies face fewer legal complications, regulatory hurdles, and financial penalties. This reduces operational risks and increases profitability in the long run. When a company upholds ethics, its financial stakeholders—whether they are shareholders, banks, or private equity firms—have confidence in its stability, ensuring a steady flow of capital and investment.

Employee retention is another key benefit of ethical business conduct. Organizations that prioritize ethical leadership and workplace fairness tend to have lower attrition rates, as employees feel valued and secure. Also, ethical companies foster stronger workplace cultures. Employees experience higher job satisfaction, motivation, and productivity, and they take pride in their work because they are part of something credible. Furthermore, the sense of security in working for a company that operates with fairness and transparency leads to higher efficiency. When employees trust their leadership, they align their personal growth with the company's success.

The reality is simple—ethics is not an optional strategy; it is the backbone of sustainable business. The world's most respected and enduring companies—Tata, Godrej, Hindustan Unilever, and countless others—did not achieve greatness through shortcuts. They built legacies through integrity, transparency, and a commitment to ethical leadership. Whether in business, leadership, or life, the long road of ethics always leads to the strongest foundation.

Short-term gains may seem tempting, but in the grand scheme of things, only ethical businesses create lasting impact, financial success, and an enduring legacy.

In contrast, companies built on unethical practices often find themselves trapped in legal battles, regulatory scrutiny, and reputational damage. These distractions drain time, energy, and resources that could have been used for innovation and growth. Worse, unethical businesses create toxic workplace cultures, where fear and uncertainty replace loyalty and motivation. Employees hesitate to take ownership of their roles because they know the foundation is shaky. Eventually, such companies either implode or struggle to stay afloat, relying on desperate measures to sustain themselves.

India's business landscape has witnessed firsthand the consequences of ethical and unethical business practices. Some companies soared to extraordinary heights, only to crumble under the weight of their own malpractices. Their stories serve as cautionary tales, reinforcing the core message of this chapter: ethics is the bedrock of enduring businesses.

Consider the case of Satyam Computer Services. At the dawn of India's IT boom, Satyam emerged as a shining star, captivating investors and dominating the industry. But as its founder's greed took over, the company's fate was sealed. What began as an innovative IT powerhouse turned into one of the biggest corporate frauds in Indian history. The chairman orchestrated a massive financial deception, inflating revenues and siphoning off nearly ₹7000 crore into unrelated ventures like real estate.

For years, this fraudulent success story dazzled stakeholders—until the inevitable collapse.

The deceit was uncovered by auditors and bankers, and as the scandal unraveled, Satyam's reputation was destroyed. Investors, employees, and banks lost all trust, and the once-flourishing company went bankrupt. Its founder landed behind bars, his name erased from India's corporate memory. The remnants of Satyam were eventually acquired by Tech Mahindra, marking an end to one of India's most infamous financial scandals. Even after the acquisition, Mahindra distanced itself from Satyam's tarnished name, rebranding the entity as Tech Mahindra to ensure a fresh start.

A more recent example is Yes Bank. At its peak, Yes Bank was an industry disruptor, giving stiff competition to established banking giants like State Bank of India and Punjab National Bank.

Its meteoric rise was led by its charismatic founder, Rana Kapoor, a seasoned banker with international experience. His vision was to build a customer-friendly, high-growth financial institution—and for a while, he succeeded.

However, unchecked ambition turned into greed. Kapoor indulged in high-risk lending, offering substantial loans to companies with questionable repayment capacities, all while pocketing hefty kickbacks. His strategy was simple but dangerous: rapid expansion fueled by reckless credit disbursal. The result? A staggering ₹3277 crore in bad loans, creating a financial black hole that even the Reserve Bank of India (RBI) couldn't ignore.

When Yes Bank collapsed under the weight of its own mismanagement and unethical financial practices, the Reserve Bank of India (RBI) had no choice but to step in. When the RBI stepped in, an audit exposed the depth of the mismanagement. The truth was unavoidable—Yes Bank was on the brink of collapse. The crisis wasn't just about one individual's fall from grace—it was about protecting millions of depositors, businesses, and employees who had placed their trust in the bank. Unlike private corporations, where failure leads to bankruptcy, a bank's collapse shakes the very foundation of the economy. It had to be rescued.

But who had the financial muscle to take over such a massive burden? No private player could readily infuse ₹8,000-₹10,000 crores to stabilize the bank. To protect public funds and prevent a banking crisis, the government intervened. The responsibility fell on the State Bank of India (SBI). As India's largest and most trusted bank, SBI stepped in, took control, and spearheaded a financial restructuring that prevented a full-scale banking catastrophe. Today, while Yes Bank continues to operate, its majority stake remains under SBI's control, ensuring stability and trust. Rana Kapoor, once the celebrated face of Yes Bank, was arrested for money laundering. His empire, built on deception, crumbled overnight.

Now, imagine the irony—Rana Kapoor, the man who once helmed this meteoric rise of Yes Bank, a former executive at Bank of America with years of international banking experience, found himself behind bars. At the peak of his success, Yes Bank had over 1,000 branches across the country, aggressively competing with established institutions like SBI and Punjab National Bank. His customer-friendly approach initially won him accolades. But greed is a silent predator.

I had even interacted with Rana Kapoor at an industry event. As part of the Faridabad Industry Association, I had the privilege of inviting him as a guest speaker at our annual general meeting. He was confident, charismatic, and ambitious. I remember him saying, "I'd be happy to address your forum, but I'd also like to get major corporate accounts from the association." At that moment, I saw a businessman focused on growth and networking. What I didn't see— what none of us saw—was the deception brewing beneath the surface.

The Fall of a King: Vijay Mallya's Downfall

If Kapoor's story was one of silent deception, Vijay Mallya's was a spectacle of extravagance and arrogance. The man who was once celebrated as the 'King of Good Times.' His Kingfisher Airlines wasn't just a business; it was a statement. It was meant to redefine luxury travel in India.

But aviation is a brutal industry. Profitability is razor-thin, and operational costs are massive. Even well-established airlines struggle. Mallya, blinded by his own ambition, thought he could outspend the competition. He borrowed heavily, believing that aggressive advertising and premium services would eventually turn the airline into a market leader. But the numbers never added up. The airline bled money, employees went unpaid, and debts ballooned.

When reality hit, and banks started demanding repayments, Mallya did what many corporate fraudsters do—he fled. In 2016, sensing legal trouble, he escaped to the UK, leaving behind unpaid loans exceeding ₹9,000 crores. The Indian government has been fighting for his extradition ever since. Meanwhile, his assets—luxury cars, sprawling mansions in Mumbai, Goa, and Bangalore, and even his prized collection of rare automobiles—have been seized and auctioned. The man who once owned more than 100 luxury cars had to watch as banks towed them away, piece by piece.

Mallya's story is a textbook case of how unethical business practices, financial mismanagement, and unchecked ambition can destroy an empire overnight. He had everything—money, influence, and opportunity. But instead of building a legacy, he chose deception. And today, he's a fugitive, facing charges of money laundering, fraud, and financial misconduct. Even now, the legal battle for his extradition continues. The British legal system operates differently, making the process slow and complex.

However, with India's growing international influence and the Prime Minister's firm stance on financial fugitives, it's only a matter of time before Mallya faces the consequences of his actions.

These cautionary tales illustrate a fundamental truth: *businesses built on ethical foundations stand the test of time, while those driven by greed inevitably collapse.*

Companies that prioritize ethics—like Tata, Infosys, and Hindustan Unilever—continue to flourish, earning unwavering trust from stakeholders. They prove that ethical business practices aren't a constraint; they are a competitive advantage.

In our own journey, we faced similar challenges. When we wanted to enter the institutional business, we encountered pressures to pay commissions and bribes. Many companies took this route, but we refused. It took us years—15 to 20 years, in fact—to establish ourselves without succumbing to unethical shortcuts. But today, we stand stronger than ever, with an untarnished reputation and a business built to last. We win contracts not because of backdoor dealings but because of our track record of excellence, integrity, and quality products at a reasonable price.

Ethical decision-making builds an unshakable foundation. Investors are drawn to transparency. Public issues get oversubscribed many times over because people trust ethical organizations. When Ratan Tata spoke at AGMs, investors did not just hear words; they heard a commitment to principles. The Tata brand's ability to attract investors, customers, and employees alike is rooted in this trust.

Beyond financial gains, ethical practices enhance a company's brand value. Government officials respect businesses that operate with integrity. Regulators scrutinize less when they know a company is above board. My company, despite being in a highly regulated industry, has never faced undue legal troubles.

We do not evade taxes, we do not manipulate accounts, and we do not engage in unethical competition. The result? Peace of mind. Reduced legal risks. An environment where employees focus on innovation and growth rather than firefighting crises born out of dishonesty.

A company's most valuable asset is its people. Ethical leadership creates an environment where employees feel secure, motivated, and proud of their workplace.

When employees know their company operates with integrity, they carry that confidence into every client meeting, every negotiation, and every deal. It empowers them.

It makes them productive, engaged, and, most importantly, loyal.

Over the years, I have come to see that ethical business is not just good business—it is the best business. It requires patience, perseverance, and at times, an unyielding stand against the tide. But in the end, it builds an empire that is not just profitable but also respectable and enduring.

My journey has been a testament to this philosophy, and as I look to the future, I am certain that the greatest legacy a business can leave behind is not just its revenue, but the integrity with which it was built.

The collapse of Satyam Computers due to financial fraud, the downfall of Yes Bank due to governance failures, and the bankruptcy of Kingfisher Airlines due to mismanagement and financial misconduct are stark reminders of the long-term risks associated with unethical behavior.

These companies initially thrived but ultimately crumbled under the weight of their dishonest practices, leading to financial losses, legal battles, and tarnished reputations.

The Power of Ethical Business

Ethical decision-making extends beyond internal operations to dealings with external stakeholders. In industries where bribery and commissions are common, companies that choose to maintain integrity face initial challenges but ultimately emerge stronger. For example, businesses that resist payments and instead invest in transparency and compliance will build credibility, attract responsible investors, and mitigate legal risks.

That's why, even as a mid-sized company with a ₹300 crore turnover, we decided to take a different path. We understood that financial integrity is non-negotiable. If you want sustainable growth, you need accountability. That's why we chose to get our accounts audited by Ernst & Young (E&Y), one of the world's most reputable auditing firms.

Typically, firms like E&Y don't work with smaller companies—we simply don't match their fee structures or scale. But I was determined. I told them, "Catch us young. We're going to grow. Partner with us now, and we'll build something together." After multiple discussions and negotiations, they agreed. Today, E&Y audits our books.

This decision isn't just about financial audits—it's about credibility. The moment a globally recognized firm puts its stamp on our balance sheet, we gain trust. Investors, stakeholders, and partners don't need to second-guess our numbers. They know that if Ernst & Young is involved, everything is transparent and legitimate.

At the time that I'm penning this down, about five of their (E&Y) auditors have been working in our office for over a fortnight. Every financial detail is being scrutinized, and every number is being validated. It's a rigorous process, but we welcome it.

Because true growth isn't about inflating numbers—it's about building something that can withstand the test of time.

Even our employees feel the impact. We have three Chartered Accountants working in our head office, and I asked them, "Are you finding this process difficult?" Their response? "No, sir. We're learning things here that we wouldn't have learned anywhere else." That's the power of doing business the right way.

At the end of the day, the difference between success and failure in business isn't just about strategy or market conditions—it's about integrity. Ethical businesses may not always grow as fast, but they grow sustainably. They don't collapse under the weight of fraud. They don't leave behind ruined investors, unpaid employees, and shattered trust.

So, when you build a company, build it with ethics at its core. Because in the long run, ethics aren't just good business—they're the only way to build a business that lasts.

The impact of ethical decision-making extends beyond profitability. It shapes the culture of an organization, influencing how employees conduct themselves and how they interact with customers and partners. Employees in ethical companies feel a sense of pride and confidence in their work. They don't have to hide anything or fear exposure because they know they are part of something honorable. This translates to higher job satisfaction, better productivity, and stronger loyalty. The benefits of ethical business practices are evident in every aspect of operations. When ethics are ingrained in a company's DNA, they become second nature. Leaders don't have to enforce them—they are simply a way of doing business. And when that happens, success follows naturally. Ethical businesses don't just build profits; they build legacies. And in the end, that is the true mark of a great company.

6

Fair Play

Competing with Integrity

"In looking for people to hire, look for three qualities: integrity, intelligence, and energy. And if they don't have the first, the other two will kill you."

— Warren Buffett

The roar of the competitive market is deafening, and in the chaos, the lines between cut throat tactics and fair play can blur. Yet, some have not only survived but thrived with their integrity intact. In the heart of the marketplace, integrity is both a shield and a sword. This chapter explores how businesses can rise above the fray with competitive strategies that honor their values, build brand loyalty, and sustain growth, all without compromising their ethical foundations. It is an ode to the art of competing with grace, a testament to the power of playing fair.

In the world of business, success is not just about being the fastest or the cheapest—it's about being trusted. The companies that endure are those that build a competitive advantage rooted in integrity.

Customers may be drawn to a lower price or a flashy marketing campaign, but what keeps them coming back is trust.

Trust in quality. Trust in consistency. Trust in a company's commitment to doing the right thing.

Take the pharmaceutical industry as an example. In the generic medicine business, affordability is a major factor. Patients often opt for lower-cost alternatives, but there's one condition—effectiveness. No one is willing to gamble with their health. A medicine that delivers results earns patient confidence. That confidence translates to brand loyalty, and loyalty is what builds a sustainable business. The reason names like Crocin and Brufen have remained household staples isn't just pricing—it's because they work. They are reliable. They have a reputation that has been built over decades, and that kind of reputation cannot be bought—it must be earned. This pattern plays out in every industry. Sensodyne became the go-to toothpaste for people with sensitive teeth, not because it was the cheapest, but because it delivered on its promise. Chyawanprash, once just another Ayurvedic formulation, became a household name because of the trust built over multiple generations of families. Brands that commit to quality and honesty create not just customers, but believers.

Innovation and Ethical Competition

It's easy to assume that staying competitive means cutting costs at any expense, but the smartest businesses understand that true competition is about more than price. Innovation, quality, and a deep understanding of customer needs are the real game-changers. The rise of e-commerce provides a perfect example. Amazon didn't just offer lower prices—it offered convenience, trust, and an ecosystem designed around customer satisfaction. By 2024, Amazon's Indian operations had generated revenues of 254 billion Indian rupees.

That kind of dominance wasn't built on price wars—it was built on service, reliability, and trust. Closer to home, Indian companies like Tata, Infosys, Wipro, Mahindra & Mahindra, and Amul have expanded their reach not just within the country but globally.

Their formula? Ethical business practices, quality assurance, and a long-term vision. They didn't seek quick wins. They built brands that people trust.

The Pitfalls of Unethical Competition

Many companies, in their race to outdo competitors, fall into unethical traps. They slash prices recklessly, mislead customers with exaggerated claims, or compromise on quality. What they fail to see is that these shortcuts come at a cost—lost credibility, declining customer loyalty, and eventual downfall. A case in point is the dairy industry. Brands like Mother Dairy and Amul have long competed in a commoditized market where milk is sold at similar prices.

Customers typically choose based on availability rather than brand preference. However, new entrants like Country Delight and A2 Milk disrupted this market by offering fresh, organic milk from well-fed cows. By highlighting superior quality and health benefits, these brands carved out a niche, attracting health-conscious consumers willing to pay a premium.

The wheat flour industry followed a similar trajectory. Once a basic commodity, wheat flour was rebranded into specialized offerings—whole wheat flour, high-fiber variants, even diabetic-friendly flour. By recognizing shifting consumer preferences, brands introduced premium products at higher price points, capturing market share while maintaining profitability.

The Power of Market Disruption

Sometimes, the most effective way to compete isn't by playing the existing game—it's by changing the rules entirely. No company demonstrated this better than Reliance Jio. When Jio entered the Indian telecom market in 2016, it didn't just offer cheaper data plans—it revolutionized the entire industry. Free voice calls. Ultra-low-cost data services. It was an unprecedented move that forced established players like Airtel and Vodafone into survival mode. Millions of users switched overnight. Competitors scrambled, some collapsed, and Jio emerged as an industry leader.

But Jio's success wasn't just about low prices. It was strategic. The company bundled its services—Jio TV, Jio Cinema, affordable 4G handsets—creating an ecosystem that locked in customers. It wasn't a race to the bottom; it was a redefinition of what telecom services could be.

Companies that commit to quality, innovation, and long-term trust don't just survive; they thrive. They build loyal customers, strong reputations, and businesses that stand the test of time.

Price wars are short-lived. Misleading marketing backfires. But trust? Trust is an asset that appreciates over time. And in a world where consumer choices are expanding every day, it's the businesses that operate with integrity that truly win.

In business, shortcuts can be tempting. The pressure to outperform competitors, maximize profits, and dominate the market can lead even the most promising companies to take the wrong path. The price of unethical competition is high—often catastrophic. The story of Byju's serves as a powerful reminder that no matter how high a company rises, a lack of integrity can bring it crashing down.

Byju's: The Education Giant That Lost Its Way

Byju's was once the darling of India's edu-tech revolution. A company that promised to transform education, helping students prepare for competitive exams with innovative learning methods. At its peak, it was a leader, attracting millions of students and billions in investment. But then, cracks began to show.

Under pressure to maintain its rapid growth, Byju's started aggressively selling expensive courses, using high-pressure sales tactics that left families financially burdened. At the same time, the company went on an acquisition spree, buying firms like Aakash Educational Services without a solid integration plan. The result? A bloated, debt-ridden organization with mounting losses.

Investors, once eager to back Byju's, started pulling out. Layoffs followed, trust eroded, and its once sky-high valuation plummeted. Today, the company, once seen as invincible, is fighting for survival.

Byju's downfall teaches an important lesson: growth at all costs is a dangerous game. Unchecked ambition, poor financial planning, and unethical business practices create a fragile empire—one that can collapse under its own weight.

The Common Thread: Greed, Mismanagement, and Broken Trust

We talked about a lot of companies that have started big, but failed soon after—Kingfisher Airlines, Byju's, Yes Bank, and Satyam Computers. What do all these companies have in common? A lack of transparency, poor governance, and overconfidence. They made the same mistakes:

1. **Misrepresentation of financials:** Inflating numbers to impress investors and stakeholders.

2. **Uncontrolled expansion:** Growing too fast without a sustainable plan.
3. **Debt mismanagement:** Relying too much on borrowed money without ensuring profitability.
4. **Ignoring ethics:** Choosing short-term gains over long-term trust.

These failures serve as stark reminders that business isn't just about profits—it's about sustainability, trust, and responsibility.

India is an extraordinary battleground where businesses, both large and small, have forged their journeys on the sacred soil of enterprise. The country has been a launchpad for some of the world's most formidable brands, proving time and again that ethical competition is not just a virtue but a winning strategy. Ethical businesses don't merely survive; they thrive, setting benchmarks in innovation, customer trust, and long-term sustainability.

One of the finest examples is Amul, the dairy cooperative that revolutionized the industry in 1946. Instead of merely capitalizing on the market, Amul built an ecosystem that empowered farmers, trained them in quality standards, and provided them with additional income. The result? A dairy giant that didn't just dominate India but also made its mark in global markets with an unshakable supply chain. This is the power of ethical business—growth driven by empowerment and value creation, not exploitation.

Then comes Patanjali Ayurveda, a brand that disrupted the FMCG sector in ways that multinational giants like Hindustan Unilever, Nestlé, and Godrej never anticipated. Baba Ramdev, a yoga guru with no prior business background, transformed traditional Ayurvedic products into a nationwide movement. By championing the idea that consumers should support indigenous brands—"buy Indian, support Indian economy"—Patanjali carved out a massive loyal customer base. The response was so seismic that the industry leaders had no choice but to launch their own natural and Ayurvedic product lines. Here lies the lesson: ethical disruption leads to industry-wide evolution.

Another homegrown success story is the Shahnaz Husain Group, which pioneered Ayurvedic beauty solutions as early as 1970, long before "clean beauty" became a global trend. Competing with multinational giants, Shahnaz Husain built a brand rooted in authenticity, catering to the evolving consciousness of consumers who sought herbal and chemical-free alternatives. Today, it stands as an iconic Indian brand, trusted by millions worldwide.

If ethical competition were a passing trend, companies like Tata, Reliance, Infosys, and Wipro wouldn't have scaled the heights they have achieved. What makes them different? Their ability to balance aggressive growth with ethical governance, timely diversification, and financial prudence. By embedding ethical practices into their core strategies, they've not only created wealth but also inspired trust—something that no marketing budget can buy.

The Business Imperative: Why Ethical Competition Matters

Innovation, reputation, and fair play aren't just abstract ideals; they're real-world strategies that build lasting businesses. Take India's infrastructure revolution, led by the visionary Shri Nitin Gadkari. When he took charge, road development was synonymous with cost overruns, subpar quality, and endless delays. The conventional practice of awarding tenders to the lowest bidders had crippled the sector. Gadkari changed the game—contracts were now awarded based on capability, ethical standing, and proven expertise, not just cost.

This shift saw ethical, competent companies like Larsen & Toubro (Delhi-Meerut Expressway, Mumbai-Nagpur Expressway), GMR Infrastructure (Delhi Airport, Hyderabad-Vijayawada Expressway), and IRB Infrastructure Developers (Mumbai-Pune Expressway, Ahmedabad-Vadodara Expressway) take the reins.

The result? India now boasts world-class highways and airports that rival global standards, built not by the cheapest bidders but by the most capable hands. If there's one takeaway from these stories, it's this: ethical competition is not a constraint—it's a catalyst.

Companies that uphold ethical standards don't just attract loyal customers; they inspire trust among investors, employees, and partners.

Studies consistently show that businesses with strong ethical foundations outperform their peers in profitability and longevity.

For instance, a study by the Ethisphere Institute found that the world's most ethical companies outperform the market by 13.6% over five years. Another study by Harvard Business Review highlighted that companies with high ethical standards see greater employee retention, higher customer trust, and improved financial resilience. As an industrialist, every investment, every procurement decision, and every competitive strategy should be guided by more than just cost.

Choosing suppliers, partners, and contractors based on ethics and capability rather than just price ensures long-term success. Ethical competition is not about playing fair for the sake of morality alone— it's about building a business that stands the test of time.

In a world where reputation is currency, ethical competition isn't just an option; it's a necessity.

How We Built a 300-Crore Business Without Cutting Corners

We started as a prescription-based company. A simple process—doctors prescribed our medicines, patients bought them from chemists, and we built our business on trust. Back then, the landscape was dominated by multinationals, with only a few Indian companies in the mix. We were one of them.

But then, things started changing. The market got crowded, competition got fierce, and ethics became the first casualty. Indian companies, eager for rapid growth, began offering doctors expensive incentives—free foreign trips, airfare for family vacations under the guise of medical conferences, and under-the-table perks. It became an open secret.

By 2005-2006, this "new normal" was everywhere. And we had a choice to make.

We examined it from every angle. The numbers were clear—if we didn't follow suit, we'd lose ground. But the ethics of it? That was even clearer. We would not go down that path.
The price of our decision? Zero growth.

For two years, our business stood still. No expansion. No new opportunities. And the worst part? Everyone around us kept telling me, *"This is just how things work! Everyone does it. You should, too."*

I wrestled with it. The idea of siphoning funds, hiding transactions under fake invoices, and withdrawing cash through backdoor channels—it felt like a house of cards, waiting to collapse. More than that, it just wasn't us.

So, instead of bending to the system, we built a new one.

We saw an opening in the market. Cipla introduced a generic business model in 2006, where the MRP was high, but the selling cost was low.

Many doctors, especially those running their own clinics or hospitals, were buying generics directly. It was uncharted territory for us, but we took the plunge.

The first year was tough. We had to unlearn, re-learn, and fight for every inch. But slowly, things started to shift. The quality of our products spoke for itself. Doctors trusted us—not because of vacations, but because of results.

Then came our next move—government supplies.

We started working with the Indian Railways, the Indian Army, ESI hospitals, and Tata Memorial Cancer Hospital—institutions that valued transparency, reliability, and quality. There were no shady deals or ethical dilemmas—just business built the right way.

And then the turnaround happened.

Today, our generic business alone stands at ₹220 crores per annum. We don't even operate across the entire country yet, and we're already competing neck-to-neck with the industry giants.

The best part? We built this with a clear conscience. No shortcuts. No compromises. Our team is motivated, our organization is driven, and our reputation? Untouchable.

Yes, ethical competition takes longer. It's harder. But when you win, you win big. And you never have to look over your shoulder.

Ethical competition and brand loyalty aren't just buzzwords—they're the backbone of sustainable success. When brands engage in ethical practices, they build trust, and trust is the cornerstone of loyalty.

We've all seen it—brands making outrageous claims like *"Grow your hair in 7 days"* or *"Get fairer in 10 days."* Have you ever seen a medicine, formula, or supplement that can do that? Yet, some brands are built on these illusions—showing a darker complexion on one side of the packaging and a magically fairer one on the other.

We never did that.

Because we know it's not just unethical—it erodes trust and is also not possible. Customers aren't fools. They see through manipulative tactics. And when a brand lies once, consumers never believe them again.

Our brand, Piltop-DSR, became a market leader because we stuck to honesty. But then came the *'Abibas'* and *'Nikke'* copycats of our brand. Hiltop-DSR with the same packaging and same colors, almost identical branding. We fought them in the Indian courts, in the trademark and copyright offices, but the battle never ends.

Yet, there's a reason customers stick with us. They recognize authenticity. They see who's playing fair and who's just riding on someone else's success. People want to be loyal to brands that stand for something real.

Some companies try to win through underhanded strategies—hiring temporary workers to cut costs, sacrificing product quality, and focusing on short-term gains. But these tactics always backfire in the long run. When you manipulate, you get one sale. When you're ethical, you build a lifelong customer.

How Ethics Build Empires

The Fab India Case: One of my favorite examples of ethical business success is Fab India. What started as a small initiative by John Bissell, an American working for the Ford Foundation, became a retail giant with 357 stores in 127 cities and 13 international outlets. Their revenue in 2022-23? ₹1,688 crores.

How?

By supporting artisans, promoting fair trade, and staying true to traditional Indian crafts. They didn't just sell clothes; they empowered rural weavers and craftspeople.

Their business model wasn't built on deception—it was built on trust, sustainability, and authenticity.

If you walk into a Fab India store, you don't feel like you're being sold to. You feel like you are part of something bigger. That's what ethical competition does. It creates real connections.

Ethical competition isn't just a feel-good concept—it's a strategy that works. And some of India's greatest business leaders have proved it.

Take Ratan Tata. Under his leadership, the Tata Group refused to engage in corruption, even at the cost of losing lucrative deals. They walked away from contracts that required unethical compromises—something few other companies dared to do.

Then there's Narayan Murthy of Infosys, Kiran Mazumdar-Shaw of Biocon, and Azim Premji of Wipro—leaders who built billion-dollar businesses on transparency, accountability, and fair play.

At the end of the day, business isn't just about making money. It's about making money the right way.

We made our choice years ago. We built a business without cutting corners. And today, we're stronger for it.

Win the customer's trust, and you win the market.

The Lessons We Must Learn

What does it take to build an ethical business? What's the first step toward ensuring that a company's competitive strategy aligns with ethical standards? If you ask me, it all begins with a dharma—an unshakable foundation of principles that guide every decision, every action. For businesses, that dharma takes the form of a Code of Ethics. Think of it as the *Gita* for an organization—providing wisdom, clarity, and a moral compass that must be followed, no matter how tempting the shortcuts.

The corporate world is full of temptations to take shortcuts, but history shows that ethical businesses stand the test of time. Companies that prioritize transparency, governance, and ethical decision-making build credibility. And credibility, once lost, is nearly impossible to regain.

In the long run, only businesses that create competitive advantages survive by securing better pricing and profitability. However, maintaining ethical standards is crucial in this process. Fair business practices and ethical conduct foster customer trust, leading to repeat purchases and long-term brand loyalty. Especially in the pharmaceutical industry, while affordability is a significant factor, the most crucial aspect is good quality and effectiveness. Customers seek savings, but not at the expense of efficacy. When medicines deliver reliable results, patients develop trust, leading to repeat sales and a strong brand reputation over time. Businesses can build competitive advantages through innovation while maintaining ethical standards. One key strategy is addressing societal shifts and consumer needs. The rise of e-commerce exemplifies this trend.

Many companies become overly focused on outpacing their competitors, often neglecting to consider customer preferences and needs. This short-sighted approach leads to dissatisfied customers and diminished brand loyalty. A common pitfall is engaging in price wars, where companies aggressively lower prices to gain market share. However, such strategies rarely translate into sustainable growth and often erode profit margins.

Instead of engaging in destructive price competition, businesses should prioritize innovation, customer benefits, and superior products and services. Understanding customer needs and market trends allows companies to develop differentiated offerings that build long-term loyalty.

Another effective strategy is market disruption through innovative business models. A prime example is OYO Rooms' disruption of the budget hotel industry. Founded in 2013, OYO identified a major gap in the hospitality sector: the lack of standardized and reasonably priced accommodations. Instead of developing its own hotels, OYO collaborated with small, unbranded hotels to standardize the consumer experience by ensuring consistent amenities, cleanliness, and pricing under the OYO brand.

OYO grew quickly in India and then internationally, thanks to aggressive technological integration, such as mobile booking, dynamic pricing, and property management systems. This tech-driven, asset-light strategy upended established hotel chains and changed the Indian budget travel market by providing millions of budget-conscious tourists with transparency, reliability, and accessibility.

These practices highlight that ethical competition does not mean avoiding aggressive strategies. Instead, businesses should leverage innovation, product quality, and consumer-centric solutions to gain a competitive edge while maintaining integrity. Ethical businesses foster trust, build sustainable brands, and achieve long-term profitability.

At the end of the day, what truly sets a business apart isn't just strategy, market dominance, or profitability—it's the ethical backbone that holds it all together. Without it, even the most successful companies can crumble under the weight of their own unchecked ambitions.

So, what's the first step toward building an organization that stands the test of time? Simple: establish a code of ethics—a guiding light that ensures every decision, big or small, is rooted in integrity.

Every new hire should read it, absorb it, and understand that this is not just a document—*it's the foundation of how we operate. This is what we stand for. This is what we will never compromise on. And most importantly, this is what we expect every single person in the company to uphold, from the boardroom to the shop floor.*

But a code of ethics alone isn't enough. Leadership must breathe life into it. Ethical leadership isn't just about setting rules—it's about setting examples. Leaders must embody the company's values, ensuring that ethics aren't just a corporate buzzword but a way of life. If a manager tells an employee, "That sales tax officer is asking for ₹5000, just pay him and get it done," then what kind of culture are we building? No. It's better to fight legally, to refine our systems, to take the harder path—because taking shortcuts today will cost us our credibility tomorrow.

Regular ethical audits are crucial. Strategies need to be assessed and realigned if they drift away from ethical principles. Policies should be scrutinized, and if gaps are found, corrections should be made. Ethics isn't a static concept; it evolves, and so should our framework.

And then, there's the most overlooked part—stakeholder engagement. It's easy to assume we're ethical because we believe we are. But do our employees feel the same? Do our customers? Have we ever asked them? Conducting lectures and handing out booklets on ethics means nothing if employees are struggling with real-world ethical dilemmas with no guidance. If we're truly committed to ethics, we need to listen. Engage with employees, understand their challenges, and take feedback seriously.

The same applies to customers. We may think we've sold them a great product, but are they truly satisfied? Imagine this: I set out on a tour, visiting my top stockists, the ones responsible for moving ₹5,00,000 worth of product every month.

I sit down with them over a cup of tea—not as a salesman, not as a boss, but as someone who genuinely wants to hear them out. Are they happy? If not, why? Are we missing something? We may pride ourselves on being truthful and ethical, but if our stakeholders see gaps, those need to be addressed. Ethics isn't just about doing the right thing—it's about ensuring that others feel the impact of that rightness.

Another critical step: integrating ethics into strategic planning. Every business decision, every policy change, every expansion plan must consider its impact on employees, customers, suppliers, and the community. Ethics should never be sacrificed for short-term gains. Long-term value should always take precedence because ethical businesses don't just survive—they thrive.

Transparency is where most companies falter. A true ethical culture isn't one where employees are policed into compliance. It's one where they feel safe to voice concerns without fear. A company that establishes a code of ethics but never checks in with employees, never asks, "Are you facing any ethical dilemmas?" is setting itself up for failure. We need to create a culture where people aren't afraid to speak up and, more importantly, where their voices are heard.

Accountability is just as important. Ethical breaches, whether committed by a single individual or a team, can tarnish the reputation of an entire organization. That's why unethical behavior cannot be brushed under the rug—regardless of who is responsible. A strong manager doesn't look the other way; they fix the problem or remove the source of the problem. That's the only way to protect the company's integrity.

Then comes continuous learning. Ethics isn't a one-time training session. As new challenges emerge, training programs must evolve.

Employees need the tools to recognize and navigate ethical dilemmas. They need to be encouraged to think critically, to challenge questionable practices, and to understand that ethics is not a limitation—it's a strength. Compliance with legal regulations is non-negotiable. Laws and standards change constantly. The Supreme Court rules on something new, the Finance Ministry introduces a new policy—how do we stay ahead? A dedicated legal and compliance team must be in place to monitor and interpret these changes, ensuring that our company never falls into ethical or legal grey areas.

Finally, corporate social responsibility (CSR). This isn't just about meeting government mandates; it's about giving back to the society that sustains us. The law now requires companies with profits above ₹5,00,00,000 per annum to allocate 5% to CSR initiatives. But this isn't just a tick-box exercise. This is a chance to make a real difference—whether in education, healthcare, or environmental conservation. And let's be clear: CSR isn't about writing a cheque to a relative and calling it charity. It's about making meaningful contributions. If you can't find a cause, donate to the Prime Minister's Fund. But do it right. Because when a company invests in society, it doesn't just build its brand—it builds its legacy.

Ethical business isn't just a philosophy—it's a necessity. It defines who we are, how we operate, and whether we will be remembered as a company that stood for something. It's the difference between businesses that collapse under scandals and those that endure for generations. Ethics isn't just a choice. It's the only choice. A business that truly integrates ethics into its DNA will not just survive; it will thrive, earning respect, loyalty, and prosperity that endures for generations.

In the end, success is not just about how high a company climbs—but how solid the foundation is beneath it.

7

When to Pass the Baton

Timing your Exit

"The greatest leader is not necessarily the one who does the greatest things. He is the one who gets the people to do the greatest things."

— Ronald Reagan

There comes a moment in every race when the seasoned runner feels the wind shift and knows it's time to hand over the relay baton. This chapter confronts that pivotal moment in entrepreneurship—recognizing when the time has come to pass on the leadership to ensure the legacy continues.

Timely succession is an art—a strategic maneuver that secures the future of the enterprise while honoring its past. This chapter is dedicated to identifying the signs that tell it's time to transition, preparing for that transition, and executing it with wisdom and foresight. Change is inevitable. But in leadership, recognizing the right moment to step aside—or step up—can make or break an organization. I've been in the business world for nearly four decades, and if there's one thing I've learned, it's this: leadership transitions aren't just about individuals; they're about the survival, evolution, and legacy of a company. Smooth transitions don't happen by accident. They require clear, open, and two-way communication. They demand foresight, planning, and, above all, the humility to recognize when a new perspective is needed. So how do you know when it's time for a leadership change? The signs are all around you—if you're willing to see them.

1. **Declining Financial Performance:** Numbers don't lie. When revenue starts dipping, when margins shrink, and when targets become distant dreams instead of achievable goals, it's a glaring red flag. I've been at the helm for decades, but if I find myself unable to steer the financial ship as effectively as before, it's my responsibility to step back and let someone else take the wheel. A leader who clings to power while the company sinks is not a leader but a liability.

2. **Market Share Erosion:** Business is war. Every day, new competitors enter the battlefield, fighting for the same customers, the same contracts, the same limited pie. If my company starts losing significant market share, I need to ask myself: Is my strategy outdated? Am I resisting change? If I don't move, the market will move on without me. A company that fails to defend its position is a company in decline.

3. **Operational Inefficiencies:** Here's the truth: comfort is the enemy of progress. As leaders, we develop habits, routines, and ways of working that served us well in the past. But what worked yesterday may not work tomorrow. AI, automation, big data—these aren't buzzwords; they're survival tools. If I can't keep up with the technological revolution, I'm holding the company back. And the brutal reality? Inefficiency today is bankruptcy tomorrow.

4. **Resistance to Strategic Shifts:** I've seen family businesses stagnate for decades because they refused to evolve. Grandfather sold textiles, father sold textiles, and now the grandson is expected to do the same—even when the market demands innovation. The new generation, armed with global education and exposure, often has the vision that can take the business to new heights. The old guard must recognize this and make room, not resist.

5. **Merger and Acquisition Opportunities:** There's a goldmine in strategic acquisitions. Across industries, there are brilliant businesses trapped at a ₹50 crore turnover ceiling because the next generation has moved on. They work at Google in the U.S., are married abroad, and are uninterested in running the family business. This creates ripe opportunities for mergers. If leadership is unwilling to recognize these chances for growth, the company remains stagnant. In business, stagnation is the first step toward irrelevance.

6. **Stakeholder Pressure:** Stakeholders—whether investors, board members, or partners—aren't sentimental. They care about growth, profits, and sustainability. If I'm more focused on my golf game than my company's trajectory, if board meetings are filled with dissatisfaction and declining confidence in leadership, then it's a clear sign: time's up. Either I reinvest my energy into leading, or I step aside for someone who will.

7. **Employee Dissatisfaction & Attrition:** Loyal employees don't leave bad companies—they leave bad leadership. If I notice high attrition rates, disengaged teams, or open calls for change, it means I've lost touch with the people who keep the business running. Leadership isn't just about vision; it's about

connection. If employees no longer believe in the leadership, that leadership is already over.

8. **Reputational Damage & Public Scrutiny:** A company's reputation can take years to build and seconds to destroy. Scandals, financial mismanagement, or public criticism can force leadership changes overnight. I've seen CEOs ousted because they ignored internal fraud, allowed ethical violations, or simply misread public sentiment. If leadership becomes a liability to the company's brand, replacement isn't an option—**it's a necessity.**

9. **Lack of Succession Planning:** Here's the biggest mistake family-run businesses make: waiting too long. I've seen 80-year-old founders still clutching the reins, refusing to let go, convinced that no one else can do the job. This isn't leadership—it's ego. A great leader doesn't just build a company; they build the next generation of leaders. Whether it's a family successor or a talented employee, the transition should be planned, structured, and embraced—not resisted.

10. **Major Organizational Restructuring:** When companies grow, they evolve. Sometimes, that evolution requires a different kind of leadership. If restructuring is on the horizon—whether it involves new markets, products, or business models—then leadership must also evolve. If I am not the best person to lead that transformation, my duty isn't to hold on; it's to find the person who can.

Leadership is a Responsibility, not a Throne

The best leaders know when to step down. It's not about clinging to power but about ensuring the company's long-term success.

A well-planned leadership transition preserves institutional knowledge, maintains stability, and injects fresh energy into the business. I have built, led, and grown businesses, and I know this: leadership isn't about how long you stay—it's about what you leave behind. When the time comes, a true leader doesn't resist change. They drive it.

Preparation, the Secret to a Successful Succession

Succession isn't just about passing the baton—it's about ensuring the race continues with the same momentum, if not greater. It's about preserving what you've built, maintaining stability, and setting up the future leadership for success. Without careful planning, businesses crumble, legacies fade, and hard-earned reputations get lost in the chaos of leadership transitions. Here's why preparing both yourself and your business is non-negotiable.

Preserving the Legacy: More Than Just a Name

Every business is built on a foundation of values, reputation, and a unique way of operating. When we talk about legacy, it's not just about keeping the name alive; it's about preserving the DNA of what made the business successful in the first place. Take Haldiram, for example. You walk into any of their outlets, and there's an unshakable trust that the sweets are of the highest quality. Why? Because for generations, they've maintained strict parameters—where to source cashews, how to refine sugar, which standards to uphold in production.

Now, imagine a poorly planned succession where the successor lacks an understanding of these intricate details. Compromises creep in, quality dips, and soon, the very essence of the brand is diluted.

That's why succession planning isn't just about finding a new leader—it's about ensuring they inherit not just the title but the philosophy and standards that keep the business thriving.

Look at Tata. Whether it's jewelry from Tanishq or a car from Tata Motors, customers don't bargain. They know that if Tata promises 22-carat gold, it's exactly that—no deception. That trust took decades to build. The moment a successor starts making decisions solely based on cost-cutting rather than quality and ethics, the legacy begins to erode. A robust succession plan ensures the next leader understands why the business stands where it does today and how to uphold its reputation.

The most dangerous mistake in succession planning is assuming that bloodline equals capability. Too often, businesses suffer because an incapable heir is handed the reins simply because they are "family." Picture this: a second-generation business owner who shows up at 11 AM, leaves at 4 PM, spends more time at social events than in boardrooms, and resists allowing experienced professionals to step in. What happens next? Employees disengage. Customers feel the shift in service quality. Long-time stakeholders start pulling back. The empire built over decades begins to crumble, not because of external competition, but due to internal neglect.

True leaders recognize that succession should be about merit, not just lineage. Maybe the daughter is more capable than the son. Maybe the most loyal employee, who has worked tirelessly for years, is the right person to carry the torch forward. A well-planned succession isn't about emotion—it's about ensuring continuity, competence, and the least amount of disruption. A business isn't just its owner— it's the people who make it run every day. A seamless succession requires identifying the key players who have been instrumental in its growth and ensuring they stay committed through the transition.

The CFO, the production head, the top sales manager—these are the pillars holding the business together. If they feel neglected, undervalued, or insecure about their future, they will leave.

And when key talent walks away, they often take the business's momentum with them.

A strong succession plan involves:

- Early identification of critical employees.
- Offering incentives: Equity, long-term bonuses, or leadership roles—to ensure their continued commitment.
- Gradual empowerment: Handing over more responsibilities before the final transition, so they feel invested in the company's future.

Ensuring Stability and Business Valuation

What if your next generation isn't interested in taking over? It's a reality many business owners face today. The son wants to build a tech startup, while the daughter prefers a corporate career; suddenly, there's no one to carry forward the business.

In such cases, the business shouldn't collapse—it should thrive. A well-structured succession plan ensures that even if ownership needs to be transferred externally, the business remains valuable and continues to thrive. This means:

- Retaining top leadership to sustain operational excellence.
- Strengthening financial health to attract potential buyers or investors.
- Ensuring that employees have a stake in the business's growth, so they remain motivated.

A sudden leadership vacuum devalues a company overnight. But with a structured plan, even if the business is sold, it can be done at a premium, ensuring wealth preservation for all stakeholders.

How many businesses have collapsed because of internal family disputes? It starts with verbal promises—"Your elder brother will be in charge, and you two will support him."

But without legal documentation, these words hold no weight. The moment the patriarch is gone, conflicts erupt. The younger brothers feel cheated, the business enters a legal battle, and in the process, the company loses credibility, market share, and sometimes, even existence.

Proper legal formalities—including clear ownership transfer, documented responsibilities, and equitable share distribution— prevent such disasters. A handshake agreement doesn't cut it in business succession. Clarity, contracts, and compliance do.

Imagine waking up one morning and announcing, "I won't be coming to the office anymore. Here's my successor." Chaos, right? Leadership transitions don't happen overnight. They require gradual grooming, handholding, and, most importantly, trust-building within the organization.

A successor needs:

- Industry knowledge—not just theoretical but hands-on experience.
- Decision-making exposure—gradual responsibility increases before the final transition.
- Mentorship—time to shadow the current leader and understand the nuances of leadership beyond boardroom meetings.

A sudden shift creates uncertainty. A gradual transition builds confidence. Today's businesses involve multiple stakeholders, including banks, investors, suppliers, employees, and even long-term customers. If they sense instability, they withdraw. Suppliers reduce credit terms, investors seek exits, and employees begin job hunting.

A well-executed succession plan ensures:

- Stakeholders see the successor in action before the transition.
- Confidence is built through transparent communication about leadership changes.
- A seamless transition plan reassures everyone that the business will continue its trajectory.

A leader's final responsibility isn't just running the business well—it's ensuring it continues to thrive without them. Succession isn't a retirement plan; it's a legacy plan. Done right, it ensures stability, prosperity, and continued success. Done wrong, it leads to disruptions, lost value, and the collapse of everything built over decades. The choice is clear: prepare, plan, and move forward with purpose.

Selecting the Right Successor: A Leader's Legacy

Succession planning is not just about filling a seat—it's about securing the future of a company, preserving its legacy, and ensuring that the trust built over decades remains unshaken. The wrong successor can dismantle years of progress in mere months. The right one can propel the company into a new era of success. So, how do you make the right choice?

When the time comes to step down, the organization must not lose sight of its long-term mission, core values, and foundational principles. As a leader, you may have navigated the company with instinct and experience, meeting privately with finance, marketing, HR, and key clients—building relationships, setting prices, driving business forward with a one-man-show mentality.

But here's the challenge

What happens when that one-man show is no longer in charge?

Most legacy-driven businesses operate like this: The right hand doesn't always know what the left hand is doing.

The leader carries the vision in their mind, but it isn't explicitly documented or communicated. That has to change. The future leader cannot operate in a vacuum. They must know, and everyone else must know, exactly what the company stands for, where it is headed, and what is non-negotiable in its culture and values. Writing it down, communicating it across teams, and ensuring alignment are crucial. The company must not just prepare a successor—it must prepare the entire organization for a seamless transition.

Too often, leaders hold onto power until they're forced to leave, either by age, health, or unforeseen circumstances. Some continue signing checks themselves, making all the decisions, and resisting change—only to realize, too late, that they have no successor ready to step in.

The new generation is different. They are trained, educated, and often gain experience working in some organizations before returning to the family business. This is an advantage—if leveraged correctly. But you can't wake up one morning, decide to announce a successor, throw a party, and expect the transition to work smoothly.

Succession is not a one-time event; it is an ongoing process. The chosen candidate must be groomed subtly, tested in real business scenarios, and evaluated over years, not days. Without explicitly telling them they are being prepped for leadership, observe how they handle responsibility. Do they listen, understand, and execute with diligence? Are they proactive? Are they resilient under pressure? If they falter, do they learn from their mistakes or retreat? JRD Tata recognized Ratan Tata's potential early on and moved him across multiple Tata enterprises—Tata Steel and Tata Motors—over a decade before appointing him as the leader. That level of preparation is non-negotiable.

A strong leader is not just about skill—it's about mindset. When corporations promote leaders, they don't just look at experience; they put candidates through rigorous assessments, evaluating emotional intelligence, decision-making, crisis management, and adaptability. Because the truth is: when you pass the baton, you have no control over what challenges will arise next. The new leader must be prepared for anything.

Your successor must possess:

- Vision – Can they see beyond the present and anticipate future trends?
- Adaptability – Can they navigate disruptions without losing the company's core identity?
- Emotional Intelligence – Can they lead people, earn trust, and make difficult decisions without alienating stakeholders?
- Decision-Making Ability – Can they take calculated risks, pivot when needed, and stay composed in a crisis?

You won't get these answers in a single interview. You get them through years of interactions by discussing real-world business failures and gauging their responses. Even the sharpest leaders have blind spots. You may believe you've found the perfect successor—but confirmation is key. This is where external consultants play a crucial role. They provide an unbiased, scientific evaluation through psychometric tests, case studies, and group exercises. They identify strengths and weaknesses you might have overlooked.

Yes, it may cost a few lakhs to bring in these experts, but what's that compared to the cost of placing the wrong person at the helm? A single bad leadership decision can set a company back by decades.

A leader who doesn't align with company culture will face resistance at every level. Imagine a company with a 50-year-old tradition of giving employees four days off for Diwali. Then a new leader comes in and cuts it down to one. The backlash is immediate.

Culture isn't just about holidays. It's about how employees feel, how clients interact with the business, and how the brand is perceived. A leader who doesn't respect the company's cultural DNA will struggle to build trust, and without trust, leadership is doomed.

A new leader stepping in isn't just inheriting a title; they are inheriting relationships, a philosophy, and a history that employees have lived through. Transitioning leadership isn't just about skills—it's about credibility. Employees must see continuity in the successor's approach. The best way to ensure that? Have the outgoing leader mentor the successor closely. Not in theory, but in practice.

- Why were certain marketing decisions made?
- How were key client relationships nurtured?
- What was the thought process behind critical business strategies?

Document these. Communicate them. Ensure the successor not only absorbs the strategies but also the reasoning behind them. That's how legacy is preserved while still allowing room for innovation.

Employees, stakeholders, and clients must not feel blindsided by leadership change. They must be reassured that the transition is well-planned and that the company is not veering into uncertainty.

A simple but effective strategy: create a transition playbook. Outline the key steps, formally introduce the new leader, and highlight how continuity will be maintained. When employees see that the successor is following the same foundational principles with a few strategic innovations, they will respect them. That respect turns into trust, and trust is what drives a smooth leadership transition.

Handing over leadership isn't just about choosing a competent candidate—it's about securing the company's future. By defining the legacy, preparing early, rigorously evaluating leadership potential, leveraging external assessments, ensuring cultural alignment, prioritizing mentorship, and communicating the transition effectively, leaders can pass the baton with confidence.

Because ultimately, leadership is not about how well you lead—it's about how well your legacy continues without you.

The Cost of Delayed or Mishandled Succession: A Story of Lost Legacy and Leadership Vacuum

Let me tell you a story—one that plays out far too often in family businesses. A successful patriarch built an empire but never put his succession plan in writing. When he fell ill, he called his children together, pointed to the eldest, and said, "He is your elder brother. You have to accept what he says." But there were no legal documents, no formal advisors present in the room, and no structured discussion. Just emotions, assumptions, and unspoken tensions simmering beneath the surface.

Here's what should have happened: The patriarch should have called in his auditors and legal team, outlined his succession plan in front of his children, and asked, "Do any of you have concerns?" If they had, they could have been addressed right then. If they agreed, they should have signed legal documents with witnesses. This would have ensured that no one could later contest the decision.

But that's not what happened. And what followed was predictable—chaos.

1. Leadership Vacuum: When succession is unclear, confusion takes over. Employees look for guidance but find none. The eldest son, designated informally as the heir, is a deeply religious man.

He spends months in Haridwar, away from the business. When urgent decisions need to be made, the organization is left in limbo. Calls go unanswered. Meetings are postponed. Deals slip through the cracks. Who is really in charge? No one knows.

This uncertainty leads to paralysis. Key executives, once committed to the company's future, begin questioning their own. They think, *if leadership can't decide its own future, what future do I have here?* And so, they leave—taking their expertise and networks with them.

2. Talent Drain: Talented professionals in family-run businesses thrive on stability. They need to know who they report to, who makes the final call, and where the company is heading. Without this clarity, ambition turns into anxiety. When leadership is uncertain, the best employees start looking elsewhere.

And so, one by one, they leave—replacing certainty with speculation. Morale drops. Clients get nervous. Investors hesitate. Productivity declines. It's a domino effect. The once-thriving business begins to stagnate. Innovation slows. Revenues shrink. The market takes notice, and competitors seize the opportunity.

3. Power Struggles: With no clear leader, the family members start pulling in different directions. The younger siblings wait for the elder to step up, but he doesn't. Frustrations build. Factions form. Each member starts advocating for their own vision of leadership.

What happens next? Infighting. Whispered conversations in boardrooms. Secret meetings with stakeholders. Before long, what was once a united family turns into warring camps.

Lawsuits follow. Resentment festers. And soon, the business itself—once a source of pride—becomes a battleground.

4. Financial Fallout: Without a solid succession plan, financial risks multiply. Investors start pulling out. Banks become wary. Credit lines tighten. If leadership is unstable, so is the company's future.

And in today's world of disruptive businesses, hesitation is fatal.

Worse still, the legal battles drain company resources. Lawyers get involved. Court cases drag on. What could have been resolved with a well-planned estate and succession strategy now eats into the very foundation of the business.

5. The Role of Estate Planning-Securing the Future: Let's talk numbers. Say a business has a net worth of ₹2,000–₹4,000 crores. If succession isn't planned properly, that wealth can turn into a liability. Banks and lawyers now play a crucial role in estate planning, urging business owners to plan for their succession early.

A poorly handled succession doesn't just hurt a business—it destroys reputations, relationships, and futures. If you're a business leader, don't wait for fate to decide for you. The best time to plan is now. Gather your legal advisors, involve your family, consult your executives, and put it all in writing.

Because when the time comes, clarity will be your greatest asset. And a well-planned succession won't just protect your business—it will honor everything you've built. Preparing for leadership succession is one of the most critical responsibilities for any organization, whether it is a family-run business, a corporate giant, or a fast-growing startup. The stakes? Continuity, stability, and long-term growth. If done right, succession planning strengthens a company's future. If botched, it can lead to chaos, decline, and even collapse.

We've seen real-world transitions unfold in the past year—from the well-planned succession at Tata Group to Uday Kotak's strategic departure from Kotak Bank. Each example holds lessons on how leaders can ensure seamless transitions.

Lessons from the Titans: Planning for the Inevitable

Take Uday Kotak, for instance. Kotak Bank had grown into a financial behemoth with over 1,000 branches. He knew his time at the helm was finite, and his son was too young to immediately take over. Recognizing that a bank isn't a family heirloom to be casually passed down, he made a calculated move—he announced his intention to step down a year in advance. This gave him time to groom and identify the right successor, ensuring business continuity. And just a week ago, he officially stepped down, leaving a structured and stable leadership team in place.

Contrast that with the Tata Group, where the transition was almost seamless. Noel Tata was identified early, and there were no battles, no confusion—just a well-oiled transition machine ensuring the group's uninterrupted growth. The blueprint was already drawn up well in advance, avoiding any uncertainty.

For companies looking to emulate such seamless transitions, here's a strategic checklist to assess their readiness for succession.

1. Strategic Assessment: Identifying Leadership Needs

A succession plan isn't just about replacing one leader with another. It's about preparing for the future. Leaders must:

- Identify the critical leadership roles within the organization.
- Define the responsibilities of these roles in alignment with future business goals.
- Assess the skills needed for upcoming challenges.
- Analyze how leadership gaps can impact long-term strategy.

Case in Point: Reliance Industries' Disruptive Succession Strategy

Reliance Industries is a prime example of forward-thinking succession planning. For years, Reliance focused on petrochemicals, refining crude oil, and producing petrol. But leadership foresaw a turning point.

The next generation wasn't just handed the same business; instead, they were tasked with creating new verticals. Enter Reliance Jio. Mukesh Ambani didn't merely assign his children to oversee refineries.

He had a grander vision—to disrupt India's telecommunications industry. Reliance Jio launched with an aggressive strategy: free services for six months. It was a calculated burn—spending billions to gain billions. The result? Airtel and Vodafone were forced to slash prices, Tata Communications shut down, and Jio became the dominant force. This wasn't just about succession; it was about reinvention. Similarly, when his daughter took over Reliance Retail, it wasn't a minor division. She expanded aggressively, acquiring premium brand distributions, launching mass-market grocery chains, and taking on giants like Amazon. This was a leadership transition done right—with foresight, planning, and a well-executed vision.

2. Talent Pipeline Development: Grooming Future Leaders

Leadership isn't just about appointing a successor—it's about building a pipeline of capable leaders. Organizations need to:

- Identify and develop high-potential talent.
- Offer targeted training and development programs.
- Bring in external consultants to ensure best practices.
- Create opportunities for cross-functional experience and leadership exposure.

3. Gap Analysis: Bridging the Leadership Divide

Before handing over the reins, leaders must assess potential successors' readiness:

- Where do they lack expertise?
- Do they need external training or mentorship?

- Should they gain exposure in international markets or new business verticals?
- How can they be prepared to handle investor expectations, quarterly earnings, and stock market fluctuations?

A well-structured development program, including university leadership courses, strategic mentorships, and boardroom exposure, is essential.

4. Clear Succession Timelines and Transition Strategies

A well-executed succession plan includes:

- Clearly defined transition periods.
- Structured handover processes.
- Transparent communication with employees, investors, and stakeholders.
- Legal formalities such as estate planning and ownership structuring (especially in family businesses).

The Business Legacy: Planning for Longevity

A great leader doesn't just build a business—they build a legacy. That legacy is only secured when a well-thought-out succession plan is in place. Companies that approach succession as a long-term strategic move, rather than a last-minute decision, ensure not just survival but sustained success. In today's fast-paced, disruptive business landscape, leadership readiness isn't optional—it's critical. The organizations that prepare for succession with a structured, strategic approach are the ones that thrive. The rest? They risk fading into irrelevance. Leadership transition isn't just about passing the baton; it's about ensuring that the next person doesn't drop it.

A seamless transition is the backbone of long-term business success, and getting it right requires planning, patience, and precision.

I've been through it, and trust me, it's not just a checklist—it's an emotional, strategic, and business-critical process.

1. The Blueprint: A Clear Succession Plan

Let's be honest—nobody likes surprises when it comes to leadership changes. That's why a well-thought-out succession plan is non-negotiable. Identify potential candidates early, groom them, and define their roles clearly. A timeline gives clarity, accountability, and, most importantly, the motivation to grow into the role.

2. Clear and Open Communication: No Room for Guesswork

Transparency is everything. Every stakeholder—employees, partners, clients, even your lawyers—needs to be looped in. The more they know, the smoother the transition. Here's the thing—communication isn't just about talking; it's about listening. I once had a team member push back on a new strategy, saying, "This won't work." Instead of dismissing them, I listened. And guess what? They had a point! Two-way communication builds trust and ensures that your transition plan isn't just imposed—it's embraced.

You also can't just vanish overnight. Imagine telling your team, "I'm off to the African jungle for a month. Figure it out." Disaster, right? Hand-holding is necessary, and continuous feedback is key.

3. Training & Development: Bridging the Gaps

Even the best candidates will have skill gaps. That's where structured training comes in. But here's a warning—just sending them for fancy leadership courses isn't enough. I once saw an executive treat a training program as a mini-vacation.

He attended the sessions for a few hours, then spent the rest of the time sightseeing with his wife. That's why I introduced a simple rule: if you go for training, you come back and debrief. You present your learnings to the team. This not only reinforces the lessons but also ensures that the training investment delivers real value. Assign people to specific learning opportunities—be it management courses, shadowing senior leaders, or hands-on project ownership. But always, always hold them accountable for what they've learned.

4. Gradual Handover: A Step-by-Step Exit Strategy

A leadership transition isn't a one-day event—it's a process. Slowly delegate responsibilities, transfer key knowledge, and, most importantly, introduce your successor to critical relationships.

Think about it: If your business has deep government ties, your relationships built over 40-50 years hold immense value. You can't simply hand over a list of contacts and expect things to function properly. You need to personally introduce your successor to the key players and ensure they earn the same respect. It's like passing on not just your role but also your credibility.

I've seen leaders make the mistake of holding onto power too long, afraid to let go. But if you want your company to survive beyond you, you must make yourself dispensable. The transition is successful when the organization can operate independently of you.

Transitioning leadership is like raising a child—you nurture, guide, and then let them go. It's not about relinquishing control; it's about ensuring continuity. The goal isn't just to find a replacement, but to build a legacy where the company thrives even when you're not around. Plan well, communicate clearly, train effectively, and step back gradually. Do this, and your business won't just survive—it will evolve and flourish beyond you. And that, right there, is the true mark of great leadership.

The Art of the Perfect Exit

Leadership is intoxicating. The power, the legacy, the respect—it's easy to hold on for too long, unwilling to loosen the grip.

But the true test of a leader is knowing when and how to exit. Few have done it as masterfully as Shri Brijmohan Lall Munjal, the visionary behind Hero MotoCorp (formerly Hero Honda).

I had the privilege of being closely associated with some members of the Munjal family—friends of my age, with whom I have discussed the inner workings of their family business. And even as an outsider, it was impossible not to be in awe of the sheer brilliance with which Brijmohan ji orchestrated his succession.

Most business families have succession plans—on paper. But when the moment of truth arrives, egos clash, disputes erupt, and legacies crumble. Not this one. Brijmohan Lall Munjal engineered one of the smoothest family business transitions in Indian corporate history. No court battles. No family feuds. No market tremors. Instead, a meticulously planned transition where every single member walked away satisfied—a near-impossible feat in a family of four brothers, their children, and over 50 business entities.

Hero MotoCorp was already the world's largest two-wheeler manufacturer, with a vast empire controlled by the Munjal family.

With time, it became evident that the next generation needed a *clear roadmap*—who would inherit what, how wealth would be divided, and how the business would continue without disruptions. Brijmohan ji didn't wait for disputes to arise. He preempted them. He executed his plan like a grandmaster in a high-stakes chess game, ensuring that:

1. Business Integrity Was Preserved – The family empire was divided without dismantling the business ecosystem. The main company—the motorcycle manufacturing unit— was given to his direct lineage. But the parts manufacturing and ancillary businesses were handed over to other family

members, ensuring they remained financially strong while continuing to supply the main company.

2. **Wealth Distribution Was Precise and Undisputed** – This was where he showcased unparalleled strategic wisdom. Every brother, every cousin, and every family branch received a proportionate payout based on their level of business involvement. Some received ₹500 crore, others ₹1,000 crore, depending on their stake. No one felt shortchanged. No one contested the decision.

3. **Leadership Transition Was Gradual, Not Abrupt** – His son, Pawan Munjal, wasn't simply given the reins overnight. He was groomed, tested, and eased into leadership over several years. Brijmohan ji ensured that by the time he stepped back, Pawan Munjal had the respect and authority to lead without resistance.

4. **Family and Business Were Kept Separate** – The family met regularly—weekly, monthly—to discuss ownership matters in private. But professionals ran the operations, ensuring no business disruptions.

5. **No Power Struggles, No Court Battles** – In a world where even the biggest corporate houses get entangled in decades-long disputes, this was nothing short of a miracle.

When the time came for Brijmohan Lall Munjal to step back, he didn't cling on. He wasn't the eldest, but he was the sharpest. And unlike many leaders who try to control from the shadows, he made a clean break, ensuring his presence never overshadowed the new leadership.

The result?

- Hero MotoCorp continued its dominance.
- The family remained intact.

- The market remained confident.

Today, business schools must be studying this case—because it deserves a place in history as one of the most flawlessly executed leadership transitions in corporate India.

Lessons from Corporate Family Feuds

In my nearly 40 years in business, I have witnessed first-hand the devastating consequences of poorly planned succession in family-run enterprises. Time and again, powerful business empires—built with sweat, intelligence, and vision—have crumbled, not due to market forces or competition, but because the patriarch failed to plan his exit wisely. Many leaders are either emotionally afraid or simply unwilling to have honest, difficult conversations about succession. They avoid legal structures, consultants, or written agreements. Instead, they rely on vague verbal assurances like 'respect your elder brother,' 'the business stays in the family,' or 'we will decide when the time comes.' But a lack of clarity is a breeding ground for disputes. When these conversations are left unresolved, succession wars erupt, turning boardrooms into battlefields and blood relatives into bitter rivals.

Case Study 1: Ranbaxy – A Legacy Sold and Shamed

Another tragic case is Ranbaxy Laboratories, founded by Dr. Parvinder Singh. Initially, the company was a shining star in India's pharmaceutical industry, but internal mismanagement and a lack of ethical governance created serious problems. Parvinder Singh's successors failed to maintain transparency in regulatory practices, and when the cracks became too visible, the family made a desperate decision—to sell the company to Daiichi Sankyo, a Japanese pharmaceutical giant, in 2008. However, there was a hidden clause in the sale agreement: if undisclosed wrongdoings were later discovered, the sellers would be held accountable. And that is exactly what happened. Regulatory violations and fraudulent practices came to light, resulting in a multi-million-dollar legal settlement in the Singapore International Court of Justice. The Singh family was forced to liquidate assets, including their stake in Fortis Healthcare, to cover the damages. What could have been a generational empire was lost due to short-term thinking and poor governance.

Case Study 2: The Raymond Group – A Father-Son Feud

Few stories of corporate succession are as heartbreaking as that of the Raymond Group. Gautam Singhania, the current chairman, had a falling-out with his own father, Vijaypat Singhania, the man who built Raymond into a luxury brand. The elder Singhania had reportedly trusted his son to take care of the family, including the iconic Malabar Hill property in Mumbai. What followed was a legal and emotional battle that played out in full public view. Vijaypat, who once controlled a vast business empire, was left homeless, appearing in media interviews to plead for justice. The emotional toll of a poorly handled succession was evident—wealth was lost, relationships were shattered, and the once-glorious legacy of Raymond was stained.

Transitioning Out Can Be as Impactful as Leading

Leadership is often defined by the ability to inspire, strategize, and drive change. But what about when it's time to step aside? Transitioning out of leadership is an art—one that can define a leader's legacy as much as the years spent at the helm. If done with foresight and intent, stepping down can be just as impactful as leading.

I've lived through this transition myself. The process was not merely about passing the baton; it was about ensuring the organization, the people, and the legacy I built would continue to thrive without me. Here's what I learned:

1. Empowering the Successor: The True Test of Leadership

A leader's real success isn't in holding power—it's in knowing when and how to give it away. I've seen too many leaders create detailed transition plans but still retain control over the checkbook, dictate every move, and insist on final approvals. If you still have to sign off on everything, what's the point of naming a successor?

When I decided to pass the reins to my son, I took a different approach. For five to six years, we worked side by side, making decisions together, debating strategies, and aligning our visions. I had been the Managing Director, and when the time was right, the company made me Chairman, and my son took my previous role. But I didn't just hand him a title; I made sure he truly led.

Our discussions culminated in action. After aligning on a decision, I made him send the emails, take charge in meetings, and execute the plans. He wasn't just shadowing me—he was stepping into the role before it was officially his. This gradual handover ensured continuity of our company's philosophy, legacy, and culture.

People often fear young successors, especially those with foreign MBAs and bold ideas. But leadership isn't about resisting change— it's about empowering the next generation to innovate while staying anchored to the organization's core values.

2. Securing Long-Term Impact: The Leader's Legacy

Great leaders don't just build organizations; they build systems that outlive them. Defining and documenting the company's vision, values, and philosophy is critical. But it's not enough to write them down—you have to embed them into the culture. I ensured that my core team was trained not only on processes but also on behavior, decision-making, and respect for every level of the organization.

One of the biggest risks during leadership transitions is arrogance creeping into the new leader. Just because someone is now at the top doesn't mean they should forget how to engage with junior employees. Leadership is about conduct, not just strategy.

To ensure this, I organized structured transition meetings over two years. My son didn't just learn how I made decisions—he saw how I treated people, how I built consensus, and how I dealt with setbacks. Most importantly, I shared my failures. Every leader has them. How many decisions went wrong? What lessons did I learn? By sharing my mistakes, I ensured my son and the leadership team wouldn't have to learn them the hard way. That's how you create a structure and culture that thrives beyond any single individual.

3. Making the Transition a Celebration, not a Goodbye

Transitions shouldn't be whispered about in boardrooms—they should be celebrated.

When my son was ready to take over, we had a new factory inauguration. Four to five hundred employees gathered that day. As I stood before them, I acknowledged the hard work of everyone who made the factory a reality. But most importantly, I took that moment to highlight my son's role. For two years, he had been at the forefront of this project, making tough calls, facing setbacks, and ensuring execution. This was the perfect time to cement his leadership.

Instead of a quiet boardroom announcement, I told our people publicly:

> *"From today onwards, Mr. Siddharth Chawla, my son, will be the Managing Director of this company."*

The applause that followed wasn't just for me—it was for him. I saw the emotion in the faces of the 50-60 employees who had worked closely with him. They weren't just accepting him as a leader; they were celebrating him. That moment wasn't just about passing a title—it was about recognition, respect, and validation. Imagine if I had just told him in our home office, "Tomorrow, you're taking over." It would have meant nothing.

This is why the *how* of transition matters as much as the *when*.

4. Stepping Back Without Disappearing

A leader must know when to step aside—but also when to step in. The biggest mistake outgoing leaders make is micromanaging from the shadows. If you're still sending emails, overriding decisions, or questioning every move, you haven't truly let go.

My role now? Watch, guide, but don't interfere. I still work four days a week, but my involvement is strategic rather than operational. I no longer handle the daily grind—I let the new leadership steer the ship while I serve as a mentor.

And I have come to appreciate the joys of life beyond leadership. I love golf, so I moved into a home on a golf course. I travel for tournaments and spend three to four hours a day perfecting my swing. Leadership was my passion, but so is living life fully.

Think about it—how many of us have spent years postponing simple joys? Instead of spending your later years in stressful meetings and battling health concerns, imagine traveling to see your children, exploring new passions, and finally prioritizing yourself after a lifetime of prioritizing work.

This is what a true transition should feel like: smooth, empowering, and liberating—not just for the new leader, but for the one stepping down as well.

Leadership is a Cycle, not a Destination

Stepping down doesn't mean stepping away from impact. If anything, it solidifies the mark you leave behind.

Transitioning out of leadership isn't about replacing yourself—it's about ensuring that the organization, its culture, and its people are ready for the next chapter. It's about crafting a legacy that lasts long after you've played your part.

And when done right, it feels like a new season of life—both for the leader stepping back and the one stepping up.

Those who step down at the peak of their success are often celebrated, remembered for their vision, and respected for their wisdom. Look at Uday Kotak. He built one of the most formidable banking institutions in India, and yet, when he stepped down, he did so with grace. He didn't cling to power; he set a roadmap for the future and moved into a mentoring role. That's the mark of a leader who knows the value of timing.

Many leaders struggle with the idea of stepping down, fearing they will lose their relevance and influence. But waiting too long can do more harm than good. Leadership, like everything else, has a shelf life. As time passes, energy levels dip, adaptability slows, and decision-making becomes less sharp. Innovation becomes stagnant, and resistance to change increases. I have seen it firsthand—leaders who refuse to let go, holding onto power as if their identity depends on it. They push aside fresh ideas, dismiss younger talent, and resist change, all while their own ability to execute declines. Soon, whispers start: "He's not as sharp as he used to be." "His decisions aren't what they once were." "Maybe it's time for a change." And suddenly, the very people who once admired you start questioning your leadership.

There's an even greater risk in family businesses. If an 80-year-old founder refuses to relinquish power while his 60-year-old son waits in the wings, tension builds. The younger generation, full of new ideas and energy, is forced to take a backseat, leading to power struggles, disengagement, and fractured teams. Some people in the organization remain loyal to the old leader, while others align with the new leader-in-waiting. Instead of a seamless transition, you have a division. Instead of continuity, you have chaos. Stepping down at the right time doesn't just benefit the individual—it rejuvenates the entire organization. A well-timed transition injects fresh energy, new perspectives, and innovative strategies that keep the business dynamic and competitive. It builds trust in the next generation of leadership and reassures employees that the future is in capable hands.

I saw this firsthand during my own transition. As I previously stated, my son took over as Managing Director at a pivotal moment for our company. That moment wasn't just about passing the baton; it was about securing the future of the company with the full support of its people. And in that moment, I knew I had done it right.

Key Takeaways for Indian Family Businesses

If the successful and cautionary tales have one common lesson, it is this: *succession planning is not optional; it is essential.* Indian business families must abandon informal, verbal arrangements and create structured, legally sound transition plans that ensure stability.

What Must Be Done?

1. **Start Planning Early** – Do not wait until a health crisis or external pressure forces your hand. Proactive planning ensures smooth transitions.

2. **Recognize Competence Over Birthright** – The eldest son or daughter may not always be the best leader. Leadership should be about ability, not tradition.

3. Use Legal and Professional Help – Engage lawyers, consultants, and governance experts to draft a clear succession roadmap that all family members agree upon.
4. Separate Family and Business – Personal emotions should not dictate business decisions. Professional management must be prioritized over family dynamics.
5. Financial Security for All – Even if someone is not actively involved in the business, ensure they are financially secure to prevent disputes.

Many patriarchs struggle with these decisions because they involve power, wealth, and legacy—three of the most emotionally charged issues in any family. But avoiding these conversations is the worst mistake one can make.

Ultimately, a family business should not just survive—it should thrive across generations. A well-planned transition ensures not just business continuity, but also family harmony. And that is the true mark of a great leader. At the end of the day, leadership is not about how long you hold the reins—it's about how well you prepare the next generation to take over. A great leader recognizes the right moment to step aside, ensuring that their legacy isn't defined by how long they stayed in power, but by how seamlessly they passed it on.

The right time to step down is not when you are forced to, but when you can do so with dignity, confidence, and the assurance that the foundation you built will continue to thrive.

Leadership is a relay race, not a marathon—it's about knowing when to pass the baton so the race continues at full speed.

And when you step down the right way, you don't fade into the background—you become the guiding force, the mentor, the wise voice that continues to shape the organization from a place of respect and admiration. That is the true mark of a leader.

8

Training the Next Generation of Leaders

"There is nothing noble in being superior to your fellow man; true nobility is being superior to your former self."

— Ernest Hemingway

In the grand theatre of business, the spotlight inevitably shifts. This chapter highlights the critical, often overlooked act of nurturing successors—not just assigning them tasks, but also imbuing them with the vision and values that will steer the organization through new waters.

Mentorship is not just a support system but the backbone of succession planning. This chapter delves into the intentional process of developing the next generation of leaders, sharing the reins of control and the wisdom, experience, and ethical compass necessary for sustained success. Training the next generation in family-owned businesses is crucial for the enterprise's long-term success and sustainability. Family businesses often have unique traditions, values, and a legacy that make them different from others.

Training ensures that the next generation understands and upholds these principles.

A well-prepared next generation ensures a very smooth transition when the current leaders retire or step down.

Shaping the Next Generation

A great mentor is not just a guide, but a sculptor—carefully chipping away doubts, refining rough edges, and revealing the leader within. Just as Michelangelo saw David within a flawed block of marble and sculpted him with unwavering vision, a mentor must recognize hidden talent and guide it with skill and dedication. The process is neither quick nor easy—there are moments of respite among struggle, uncertainty, and even resistance. But raw potential transforms into something remarkable with time, persistence, and the proper channels. In the end, both mentor and mentee emerge stronger, forever shaped by the journey.

To me, mentorship isn't just about passing down wisdom—it's about shaping an ecosystem where experience meets enthusiasm, where the old guard and the new blood learn from each other in a continuous cycle of growth. My journey of building a mentorship culture started long before I even realized it.

Having seen firsthand how mentorship can bridge the gap between generations in family-run enterprises, I can attest to its power. The father's expectation of discipline and the son's desire for understanding can seem like insurmountable differences. The father, entrenched in routine, may wonder why his son shows up at 11 AM, while the son, exhausted from a late-night factory inspection, may struggle to explain why an 8 AM start is unrealistic. These small cracks, if left unattended, can widen into unbridgeable gaps. But mentorship has the power to overcome such differences, not with blind obedience or rigid discipline, but with structured, patient, and thoughtful guidance.

A mentor must teach, inspire, advise, and nurture. The goal is not to impose authority but to create an environment where the mentee genuinely desires to learn, grow, and eventually take the reins. In an era where young entrepreneurs often study abroad and develop an affinity for independence, the challenge deepens. Many return home reluctant to join the family business, drawn instead to the allure of foreign opportunities. If not handled wisely, what took decades to build can dissolve in a single generation. So, how does one navigate this delicate balance? The secret lies in a structured, hands-on mentorship that integrates these five essential elements:

1. **Guidance:** A mentor is a repository of wisdom accumulated through years of experience and hard-fought battles. Conversely, a mentee enters the business world armed with theory but lacking the scars of real-world challenges. The mentor's job is to provide a roadmap—illustrated with personal anecdotes, industry insights, and cautionary tales.

    I still remember when I first ventured into business. We had no money, no guidance, and no blueprint. My parents had a different trade, and I had to carve my own path. Every lesson was learned the hard way. Today's second-generation entrepreneurs won't face the same struggles, but they will encounter new ones—disruptive technology, evolving market dynamics, and changing consumer expectations. A mentor's guidance helps bridge the gap between past struggles and future opportunities.

2. **Inspiring:** Too often, mentors fall into the trap of behaving like department heads, dictating rather than inspiring. The danger of this approach? A mentee who listens out of

obligation rather than curiosity. Proper mentorship isn't about commanding respect; it's about earning it through inspiration. A successful mentor must be a living example of resilience, adaptability, and vision. Mentees should not feel shackled by the past but encouraged to challenge norms, innovate, and contribute fresh ideas. Even when those ideas seem radical, they deserve serious consideration. I have seen countless businesses thrive simply because an experienced mentor allowed a young mentee to test a bold idea rather than dismissing it outright. When mentees feel heard, they work harder, think bigger, and strive to prove themselves.

3. Sharing Knowledge: Knowledge is not just about facts and figures—it is about wisdom, intuition, and strategic foresight. The transfer of knowledge must be handled with finesse. It is not a classroom setting; it is an evolving partnership. The challenge is ensuring that the mentee hears the knowledge, absorbs and applies it. For this, the mentor must first establish credibility. Mentees must recognize that their mentor's insights stem from real-world success, failures, and reinvention. Once this mutual understanding is in place, knowledge sharing becomes an enriching journey rather than an obligatory lecture.

4. With a strong desire to mentor the next generation, I decided to support young pharmacy students in building successful careers after graduation. This aspiration led me to join the management board of the Department of Pharmacy at DAV University in Jalandhar. In this role, I contributed to designing an industry-relevant syllabus and facilitated internships in leading pharmaceutical companies, including our own, for the students. Recently, I was honored with the title of *Professor of*

Practice in the Faculty of Pharmaceutical Sciences. In this capacity, I conduct regular classes and guide students toward shaping their future with confidence and purpose. This honorary appointment has been deeply fulfilling and has allowed me to give back to the academic community in a meaningful way.

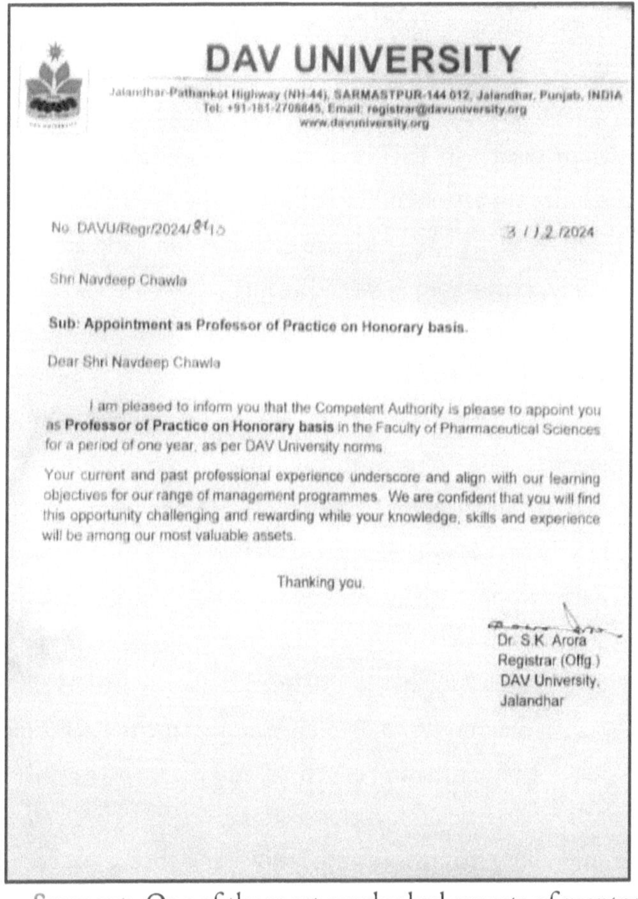

DAV UNIVERSITY

Jalandhar-Pathankot Highway (NH-44), SARMASTPUR-144 012, Jalandhar, Punjab, INDIA
Tel: +91-181-2706845, Email: registrar@davuniversity.org
www.davuniversity.org

No. DAVU/Regr/2024/8415   3 / 1 2 /2024

Shri Navdeep Chawla

Sub: Appointment as Professor of Practice on Honorary basis.

Dear Shri Navdeep Chawla

I am pleased to inform you that the Competent Authority is please to appoint you as **Professor of Practice on Honorary basis** in the Faculty of Pharmaceutical Sciences for a period of one year, as per DAV University norms.

Your current and past professional experience underscore and align with our learning objectives for our range of management programmes. We are confident that you will find this opportunity challenging and rewarding while your knowledge, skills and experience will be among our most valuable assets.

Thanking you.

Dr. S.K. Arora
Registrar (Offg.)
DAV University,
Jalandhar

5. Support: One of the most overlooked aspects of mentorship is its role in providing emotional support. Mentees, especially those stepping into leadership roles, often carry the weight of expectations. They strive to prove their worth while battling

self-doubt, external scrutiny, and internal resistance to change. The mentor's role is not just to provide constructive feedback but to build resilience and create a supportive environment.

Criticism, if not delivered with care, can be demoralizing. I have seen talented individuals walk away from great opportunities simply because they felt unappreciated. A good mentor strikes a balance between honesty and encouragement, recognizing effort as much as results. The key is to create an environment where mistakes are stepping stones, not career-ending failures.

6. **Empowering:** The ultimate goal of mentorship is not just to guide but to empower the mentee to lead. Too many businesses falter because the older generation clings to control and is hesitant to hand over responsibility. But mentorship, when done right, leads to eventual empowerment. It's a journey that starts with guidance, inspiration, knowledge sharing, and support, and culminates in the mentee taking the reins with confidence and competence.

   Early empowerment fosters confidence. A mentee who is trusted to make decisions—big or small—begins to think and act like a leader. Trust and delegation are essential. When done right, the transition is seamless; the mentor becomes an advisor rather than a supervisor, and the mentee evolves into a capable decision-maker.

I firmly believe that mentorship is not transactional (i.e., checking items off your list to 'teach' the successor)—it is a core part of legacy creation. When done right, it doesn't just build successful businesses; it creates leaders who, in turn, become mentors for the next generation. And that, perhaps, is the most rewarding outcome of all.

Back in 1987, when I started my company with barely any capital, I had just nine years of experience, most of it spent in frontline sales and later as a manager. I wasn't a veteran with decades of industry expertise, but what I had was grit, resilience, and lessons learned the hard way. Working at Ciba-Geigy (now Novartis) had ingrained in me a deep respect for transparency, integrity, and hard work. My senior managers had drilled into me a simple yet powerful philosophy—stay truthful, work relentlessly, and lead with honesty. These were more than just corporate buzzwords; they became the foundation of my company's culture. Over the years, as the business grew, so did the people in it. I take immense pride in the fact that our company has one of the lowest attrition rates in the industry. Many of our managers began their careers with us and retired after 25 years—their first and last job. That level of loyalty isn't accidental; it's a direct outcome of a strong mentorship culture.

We built an environment where people weren't just employees; they were protégés. We didn't just hire people—we nurtured them. The mentorship process was never about quick training sessions or corporate jargon; it was about embedding the company's philosophy into every interaction, every decision, and every challenge. The goal was clear: to ensure that each person, whether they joined as an intern or a mid-level manager, aligned with the organizational culture and carried forward the values that defined us. Spotting a leader isn't about scanning résumés or looking at tenure—it's about observing how someone reacts when faced with a challenge. Do they step up, or do they step back? Do they take ownership, or do they pass the buck? Do they inspire, or do they command?

In the early years, I relied on instinct. But as we grew, we needed a structured way to identify and groom potential leaders. We focused on three key aspects:

1. **Behavioral Cues Over Designations:** Leadership isn't about rank; it's about action. I've seen junior employees take more initiative than some senior managers. We closely observe how individuals interact with their peers, how they handle pressure, and how they contribute to team dynamics. Some people naturally command respect, not because of their title but because of their ability to bring people together and solve problems.

2. **Hands-On Learning with Independent Roles:** You don't learn to lead by reading a manual. We throw our potential leaders into real-life situations. We give them responsibility—real, tangible responsibility—where their decisions have consequences. Whether it's handling a critical client, spearheading a project, or managing a crisis, we let them learn by doing. Failure is part of the process, but what matters is how they handle it.

3. **Building Communication and Emotional Intelligence:** A great leader isn't just someone who knows the business inside out; they must know their people inside out. We emphasize the importance of interpersonal skills and emotional intelligence. Leadership isn't about barking orders; it's about understanding people, building relationships, and earning trust. That's why we conduct workshops, role-playing exercises, and real-time mentorship sessions to hone these skills.

4. **Encouraging Decision-Making and Risk-Taking:** One of the biggest mistakes traditional organizations make is overprotecting their emerging leaders. I've seen businesses cripple their future by micromanaging their best people. We take the opposite approach. We push them to make decisions—some small, some big. The idea is simple: if they're afraid to make decisions today, they'll never be ready to lead tomorrow.

5. **Rewarding Initiative and Recognizing Effort:** People thrive when they feel valued. We have a strong culture of recognizing those who go the extra mile. Whether it's financial incentives, public recognition, or simply a heartfelt acknowledgment, we make sure our emerging leaders know they are seen, heard, and appreciated.

Leadership isn't a title; it's a mindset. Through these techniques, we've cultivated a generation of leaders who not only work for the company but also grow with it.

The biggest challenge for any seasoned leader is knowing when to step in and when to step back. It's tempting to hold the steering wheel tightly, but authentic leadership is about knowing when to hand it over. I've seen companies struggle because their founders refuse to let go. I've also seen businesses falter because they hand over the reins too soon.

The trick is finding the right balance—a gradual transition process where guidance and autonomy coexist.

1. **Defining Roles and Setting Clear Expectations:** Clarity is everything. Ambiguity leads to confusion, and confusion leads to chaos. Before handing over responsibilities, we define roles and expectations with precision and clarity. Our emerging leaders are assigned targets and are responsible for developing their own action plans. This ensures accountability while giving them the freedom to approach challenges in their own way.

2. **Coaching, Not Commanding:** I never tell my team, "Do this because I said so." That's not leadership—that's dictatorship. Instead, I coach them by sharing my own experiences—what worked, what didn't, and why. I create an environment where they feel comfortable asking questions,

discussing challenges, and even challenging my perspective. This isn't about control; it's about guidance.

3. **Encouraging Independent Problem-Solving:** If every decision has to go through me, then I've failed as a mentor. I actively encourage my team to make decisions—whether it's a hiring call, a marketing strategy, or a customer issue. Of course, I'm there to offer insight, but I don't interfere unless absolutely necessary. This approach not only boosts confidence but also ensures they're prepared for bigger responsibilities in the future.

4. **Gradual Transition and Empowerment:** Mentorship isn't about holding on—it's about letting go, but at the right pace. As a leader, my job isn't to make myself indispensable; it's to build a team that can run the organization without me. That's why we believe in early empowerment. The sooner you give people ownership, the sooner they start thinking and acting like leaders.

At the end of the day, mentorship isn't a one-way street. I learn as much from my mentees as they learn from me. Leadership is a constantly evolving journey, and the best way to ensure a company's success is to build a culture where mentorship isn't just a program—it's a way of life.

Avoiding Pitfalls in Leadership Development

Mentoring the next generation of leaders—especially in a family business—is anything but straightforward. It's a delicate balance between experience and evolution, tradition and transformation.

Too often, founders and business patriarchs take on the mentorship role with the best intentions, only to find themselves inadvertently stalling progress rather than facilitating it.

Why? Because mentorship isn't just about passing down knowledge—it's about empowering, **adapting**, and letting go at the right time. A **successful** transition requires patience, sharp analytical skills, and a deep **understanding** of how young leaders think and operate. However, many mentorships fall into common traps that make leadership development a struggle rather than a seamless evolution. Here are the key pitfalls to avoid:

The Blind Spot – Lack of Self-Awareness: Experience is an asset, but assuming it's enough is a fatal mistake. Many senior leaders excel in execution but fail to recognize their own learning gaps. Business landscapes shift—technology advances, customer expectations evolve, and management methodologies transform. Without staying updated, even the most seasoned leaders risk becoming out of touch.

I've seen founders dismiss digital transformation, only to watch competitors leap ahead. I've seen business heads undervalue soft skills like negotiation and emotional intelligence, only to struggle with team retention. The best mentors don't just teach—they keep learning alongside their mentees, acknowledging what they don't know and embracing change.

Deaf Ears – Resistance to Feedback: In today's business world, no leader can afford to operate in an echo chamber. Organizations, especially those expanding across multiple locations, depend on listening. Take the auto industry, for example. When Honda established its first plant in India, it was located near Gurgaon. However, as demand surged, it expanded to Gujarat and Karnataka, necessitating an ecosystem of suppliers, vendors, and leadership across multiple locations. If the leadership had ignored the challenges on the ground—be it workforce issues, supply chain disruptions, or regional market dynamics—their success story could have looked very different.

Feedback isn't just a box to check—it's a growth engine. A leader who dismisses suggestions, micromanages decisions, or reacts defensively to constructive criticism stifles innovation. The reality is, you can't be everywhere—but if you build a culture where employees feel heard and valued, they'll drive the business forward in ways you never imagined.

The Fear Trap – Playing It Too Safe: Many leaders, especially in legacy businesses, fear failure to the point of paralysis. They avoid risks, fearing financial loss or damage to their brand. However, the truth is that avoiding risks is often the greatest risk of all.

The market punishes stagnation. Businesses that refuse to innovate slowly fade into irrelevance. On the other hand, leaders who take calculated risks—such as launching new product lines, investing in emerging markets, or adopting disruptive technologies—often unlock exponential growth.

The difference between failure and success isn't risk itself, but how you manage it. Great mentors teach their successors to assess risks, learn from setbacks, and turn **failures** into stepping stones.

The Missing Link – Emotional Intelligence: A leader without emotional intelligence is like a ship without a compass. You may be technically sound, but without understanding people—what drives them, what holds them back, what makes them tick—you'll struggle to build strong teams.

In family businesses, this becomes even trickier. Emotions run deep, egos clash, and unresolved **conflicts** can derail even the most promising succession plans. Successful mentorship requires empathy, self-awareness, and social intelligence—the ability to read a room, defuse tension, and inspire rather than dictate. The Communication Breakdown: You may have the best vision for the company, but if you can't communicate it clearly, it's worthless.

Poor communication leads to misaligned goals, confusion, and disengagement.

Effective leaders don't just give instructions; they inspire action. They set clear expectations, offer constructive feedback, and make sure their teams understand the "why" behind every decision. Most importantly, they foster open dialogue—where even the youngest, least experienced mentee feels comfortable speaking up.

The Change Resistance Syndrome: Change is inevitable, but many seasoned leaders resist it. They prefer what's familiar, what's "worked before." But what worked yesterday may not work tomorrow. A rigid leadership style stifles innovation. Businesses that fail to evolve—whether by resisting automation, ignoring market shifts, or adhering to outdated management styles—ultimately lose ground to more adaptable competitors. A strong mentor encourages new ideas, allows room for experimentation, and supports innovation—even when it challenges the status quo.

A true leader ensures their legacy by building leaders, not just managing employees. This is especially critical in family businesses, where succession must be intentional, not assumed. Mentorship isn't about producing clones; it's about enabling others to rise, evolve, and eventually surpass us.

How Good Mentorship Fuels a Successful Leadership Transition

Think of leadership transition like tending a garden. It's not just about planting seeds, but also about preparing the soil so that growth continues long after you've stepped away. Even the most vibrant plants can wither if the roots aren't cared for properly. Great mentorship ensures that the next gardener knows when to water, how to prune, and how to keep the garden thriving season after season.

Every business has its own DNA—a mix of strategy, culture, industry nuances, and hard-earned lessons that can't be learned from textbooks or boardroom presentations. Without a structured knowledge transfer, successors are left to figure things out on their own, often making costly mistakes along the way.

I've seen transitions where the outgoing leader assumed that simply being around the business was enough to prepare the next generation. That's a recipe for disaster. The real challenge isn't just knowing *what* to do—it's understanding *why* we do things a certain way, *when* to pivot, and *how* to think critically under pressure. That only happens when mentees are immersed in real-world decision-making, guided through both successes and failures.

The best mentorship isn't about dictating instructions but about giving young leaders the opportunity to *experience* the complexities of the business firsthand. Let them sit in on high-stakes negotiations, walk them through critical business strategies, and, most importantly, let them make mistakes while you're still there to guide them.

It's about resilience, strategic thinking, decision-making, crisis management, and people skills. The next generation must be equipped with a full spectrum of leadership abilities, from handling competition and conflict resolution to inspiring teams and executing bold strategies. The trick is to *gradually* shift responsibilities, giving them enough space to make independent decisions but being close enough to step in when necessary.

Think of it as a pilot program before they take full control. It's not about throwing them into the deep end—it's about teaching them to swim before they take the plunge. These aren't skills that can be taught in a classroom—they must be *lived.*

The best way to develop a leadership mindset is to let them shadow you. Let them see you make difficult choices.

More importantly, take the time to explain those choices. Why did you pick Strategy A over Strategy B? Why did you negotiate that deal the way you did? Why did you choose to fire or retain that employee? When mentees understand the thinking process behind critical decisions, they start developing their own judgment and strategic instincts.

Mentors who are open to questions and discussions create the strongest leaders. If mentees are afraid to challenge you, they will never develop the courage to lead in high pressure situations.

Over time, senior leaders build deep trust with key stakeholders such as clients, suppliers, employees, and investors. If these relationships are not passed on to the next generation, the business can face disruptions. Many mentors hold on to these connections, believing they are protecting the business, but in reality, they weaken their successors. Without firsthand ownership of relationships, new leaders struggle to earn the same trust and authority.

The solution is to introduce emerging leaders early. Bring them into meetings, let them handle negotiations, and give them opportunities to prove themselves. Over time, stakeholders will associate the business with new leadership, ensuring a smooth transition.

If a new leader takes over and changes the company's ethos without context, it can alienate long time employees and disrupt workflows. The best transitions happen when mentors instill core values in their successors by sharing stories, explaining traditions, and reinforcing the "why" behind the mission. Employees and stakeholders should feel that while leadership is changing, the soul of the organization remains the same.

At the heart of a successful leadership transition is trust. Trust that you have prepared your successor, that they will carry forward the business with integrity and passion, and that by stepping back, you are not diminishing your legacy but strengthening it.

Great mentorship is about empowering the next generation, not just preparing them. It is about creating a roadmap where they can take ownership, make mistakes, learn, and eventually surpass you.

A strong transition is not an end, it is the beginning of a new chapter for both mentor and mentee, ensuring the business not only survives but thrives for generations to come.

Mentoring the Successor

Mentoring a successor, especially in a family business, is no walk in the park. It's a delicate dance between legacy and innovation, between holding on and letting go. The process is layered with emotions, traditions, expectations, and, quite often, generational friction. After all, every entrepreneur who has built something from the ground up carries their struggles like a badge of honor.

I have seen it countless times—the patriarch who started with nothing, who toiled day and night, who remembers every sacrifice vividly. And then there's the next generation, raised in relative comfort, often measured against an impossible yardstick: "You don't wake up at 5 AM like I did." "When I started, I didn't even own a scooter." "You people have it easy." And in these repeated narratives, the true essence of mentorship is lost.

The reality is, mentoring is not about control; it's about enabling growth. You don't build a leader by reminding them they haven't suffered enough—you build them by giving them the tools, guidance, and trust to carry forward the vision in their own way.

Before anything else, I had to assess my successor—not just their qualifications on paper, but their temperament, decision-making ability, and leadership instincts.

Some strengths are apparent: charisma, intelligence, and technical know-how. But the gaps—those can be tricky.

I didn't expect them to replicate me, but I needed to understand where they needed refinement. Did they shy away from confrontation? Were they overconfident? Did they struggle with networking? Identifying these aspects early helped me shape my approach. I made sure my successor had access to the right technical guidance—whether through experienced employees, consultants, or specialized training programs.

But beyond knowledge, the real challenge was giving them the room to apply it. Too often, leaders cling to control, making every decision, negotiating every deal, handling every crisis. And when the successor is finally handed the reins, they are unprepared. I made a conscious effort to involve them in ongoing projects, letting them take charge of new initiatives, even if they made mistakes. Because only through hands-on experience can confidence and courage be built.

One of the biggest mistakes I've seen is sidelining successors from key decisions. Imagine working in an organization where major agreements are signed, rates are negotiated, and vendor contracts are finalized—all without your involvement. How do you expect someone to lead if they were never part of the process? I made sure my successor was included in every critical meeting. They didn't just sit and observe—they spoke, questioned, and contributed. This was not just about knowledge transfer; it was about making them feel responsible for the business's future.

It's tempting to step in and use our years of experience to solve problems instantly. A quick phone call to an old contact, a favor pulled from a retired bureaucrat—it's efficient, but it's a disservice to the successor.

Instead, I forced myself to step back. When a crisis arose, I encouraged my successor to navigate it. I was there if needed, but only as a safety net. I let them build their own network, make their own decisions, and even stumble. Because without independent problem-solving, they would never truly own their role.

One of the most overlooked aspects of mentorship is emotional support. The transition from an employee (or heir) to a leader can be daunting. There were moments my successor doubted themselves, felt overwhelmed, or made poor decisions. I had to be their anchor, offering encouragement while also pointing out areas of improvement—without breaking their confidence.

Criticism is necessary, but it must be constructive. I made sure feedback was always about improvement, never about belittlement.

If you begin at 50 and are still 'guiding' your successor when they are 40, you have failed.

A clear timeline is necessary. I set milestones—gradually shifting responsibilities, increasing independence, and stepping back. I was always available for guidance, but I ensured they had the authority to make and own their decisions. Without this structure, transition remains a theoretical exercise rather than a practical reality.

The True Measure of Mentorship

Mentorship is about trust. It's about preparing, not controlling. It's about watching your successor make decisions differently than you would and being okay with it—because their leadership is not about recreating yours, but about shaping their own.

As I look at my successor today—confident, decisive, leading the business with their own style—I know that true mentorship is not about ensuring they follow in your footsteps. It's about giving them the wings to chart their own path while carrying forward the legacy in a way that makes sense to them. And that, ultimately, is what leadership transition is all about.

I always knew I had a mind for business. Even as a college student in Jalandhar, India, the idea of running my own enterprise excited me. By the time I was in my second year of graduation, that excitement had turned into determination. I pestered my father relentlessly, convincing him to help me start a small printing press. Eventually, he relented, and in my third year, with a capital investment of ₹30,000, 'Sarvpriya Printers' came to life.

After graduation, I poured myself into the business. My daily routine was grueling—I cycled 7-8 kilometers to the press each morning, working tirelessly until 8:00 PM before cycling back home. Yet, exhaustion never overshadowed the thrill of building something of my own. My father's references helped me land printing orders from educational institutions, covering the venture's expenses. Soon, my ambition outgrew the initial success. I ventured into industries, determined to expand. A few breakthroughs came my way—product catalogues for businesses, steady contracts—but my momentum was about to be tested.

Just when things were settling, my father received a transfer order. He was to leave Jalandhar for Hoshiarpur as the principal of DAV College. With my family moving, I faced an excruciating decision: stay behind to run my business alone or join them and abandon what I had started. Initially, I tried to manage both, commuting daily between Hoshiarpur and Jalandhar. However, the 14 to 15-hour schedule each day drained me, leaving me completely exhausted. Finally, I admitted defeat. With great hesitation, I asked my parents if I could close the press and pursue further studies.

I expected resistance. After all, ₹30,000 was no small amount, and they had no idea what to do with the printing press.

But to my surprise, they simply said, "Do whatever you like." No anger, no guilt-tripping—just unwavering support. That lesson in trust and flexibility has stayed with me ever since.

So I moved to New Delhi, torn between two career paths: hotel management or becoming a Cost and Works Accountant (ICWA). Encouraged by relatives in the hospitality industry, I considered applying to IHM PUSA. But fate had other plans. I quickly enrolled in evening ICWA classes and began adjusting to my new life in the capital.

It was during this time that I met a young Kashmiri man, my neighbor in the paying guest accommodation. He was hunting for a job in the pharmaceutical industry, visiting regional offices daily, hoping to secure an interview. Listening to his stories, I grew intrigued by the medical sales field. I'm talking about a time when firms weren't giving big advertisements, and most of the offices were situated on Asif Ali Road in New Delhi. People would walk in for interviews. Fascinated by my neighbor's talks of attending interviews and discussing salary structures, I set out to do the same. On a whim, I decided to try my luck. My second interview, with Ciba-Geigy in New Delhi, changed everything. I was shortlisted for a final round in Mumbai, and before I knew it, I had landed the job.

Training lasted eight weeks. I was posted in Ludhiana and placed under the mentorship of Mr. Madan Lal. He was a seasoned professional, a relentless worker who commanded respect through sheer expertise. Over the next three years, I absorbed everything I could from him, sharpening my skills in sales, strategy, and persistence.

However, I soon felt restless. Many of my colleagues had been in the same role for years, content with the routine. But I wanted more. Stagnation terrified me.

I decided early on—I would not spend more than three or four years as a medical representative. There was no challenge left, no new learning. If I stayed, I would be stuck in a cycle with no growth.

By 1984, I was ready to take the leap. I resigned and, alongside two friends, launched a pharmaceutical marketing company. It was a bold move, one that demanded patience, risk-taking, and unrelenting effort. In 1987, I struck out on my own, founding M/s Psychotropics India Limited. It was a solitary journey at first, navigating challenges without a roadmap. Every decision mattered, and every misstep had consequences. With limited capital, I had to be meticulous—failure was not an option.

You cannot fool around and make decisions that can be detrimental to the business. You learn to move with your eyes and ears wide open and ensure not to commit any mistakes because you cannot afford it.

The growth was slow but steady. By 1989, we had acquired our first manufacturing facility. Today, my family and I run the business together—my son Siddharth and I, ensuring its legacy continues.

Looking back, I realize my path was never linear. I didn't have a single mentor guiding me at every turn. Instead, like I mentioned before, my learning came from my own experience, mostly through trials and errors and unexpected influences—a neighbor's job hunt, a father's quiet support, a mentor's work ethic. Self-learning became my greatest asset. And in the end, it was this very adaptability that built the foundation of my success. Mentorship and leadership transitions have always fascinated me—not just because of their impact on businesses, but because they shape lives, define legacies, and determine the fate of companies for generations.

My own journey has been an unconventional one, starting from a small printing press to leading a pharmaceutical company.

And along the way, I have observed and admired some of the most seamless and well-planned leadership transitions in Indian businesses.

The Lesson in Leadership Transitions

What I've learned from these two stories is simple: successful transitions don't happen by chance. They require foresight, planning, and, above all, a leadership figure who can navigate emotions, business complexities, and long-term sustainability. Whether in a family-run empire or a corporate boardroom, the principles remain the same—communication, clarity, and a vision that extends beyond personal interests. For me, having started my own pharmaceutical venture in 1987 and witnessing its growth alongside my family, the lessons have been invaluable. Transitioning leadership isn't just about passing the baton—it's about ensuring that the next runner knows exactly where the finish line is and how to get there without dropping it.Having observed the business landscape for decades, I've often wondered—what makes some leadership transitions seamless while others turn into public spectacles of conflict? What are the key ingredients of a smooth handover, especially in family-run enterprises where emotions often run high?

Through my observations and conversations, I identified five crucial factors that contributed to Hero's smooth succession.

1. Professionalization of Management

Recognizing that a sustainable business cannot rely solely on family, Brijmohan Lall Munjal brought in seasoned professionals to run the day-to-day operations. While the younger generation was given leadership roles, the real execution was managed by external experts. This separation of ownership from management ensured that even if internal family matters arose, business operations remained unaffected.

The company continued to thrive, unaffected by personal dynamics.

2. Robust Corporate Governance

One of the things that stood out in my interactions with the next generation of Munjals was the meticulous planning behind their succession. Unlike many family businesses that struggle with internal conflicts, Hero Group established clear governance mechanisms—advisory boards, decision-making committees, and external consultants like McKinsey and EY to ensure impartiality.

What truly set them apart was their respect for Brijmohan Lall Munjal, the family patriarch. Even though he was not the eldest brother, his wisdom and fairness made him the natural leader. His decisions were always rooted in the best interest of the business, not just his immediate family. This level-headed, unbiased leadership played a crucial role in ensuring a harmonious transition.

3. Core Values and Cultural Cohesion

One anecdote that has stayed with me is about the Munjal family's unwavering commitment to their traditions. I recall asking some of them to join a Sunday cricket match, and their response left a lasting impression. "We can't," they said. "Every Sunday, we go to the factory at 10 AM for a havan (prayer ceremony), followed by a family lunch." It wasn't just about religious rituals—it was about reinforcing a shared sense of purpose, discipline, and belonging. Every week, they gathered not just as a family but as business custodians, listening to speakers on ethics and moral values. This ingrained culture fostered unity, making it difficult for conflicts to arise over petty matters.

4. Balancing Tradition with Innovation

While rooted in tradition, the Munjals were quick to recognize changing market trends. Initially known for their bicycles, they saw the growing demand for motorized two-wheelers.

However, lacking the technical expertise, they sought a collaboration.

Here's where the contrast between Hero and Bajaj becomes fascinating. The Munjals approached Honda in Japan, eager to learn and partner. Honda, skeptical at first, also approached Bajaj, India's scooter giant. But Rahul Bajaj, riding high on the monopoly of Bajaj Chetak (which had a two-year waiting period!), arrogantly refused to accommodate Honda's terms. The Munjals, on the other hand, humbly agreed to Honda's guidance, signing the deal with enthusiasm. The result? Hero Honda went on to become the world's No.1 motorcycle manufacturer, while Bajaj, though still successful, lost the first-mover advantage in motorcycles.

5. Transparency in Communication and Family Unity

With a growing business empire and over 15 second-generation Munjals in the mix, clear communication was essential. Brijmohan Lall Munjal made a strategic decision—one faction of the family would handle the Hero Honda partnership, while the rest would manage other factories. To ensure fairness, he structured a financial settlement that left everyone satisfied. Instead of infighting over shares, the family members running independent businesses received substantial payouts, securing their futures while allowing the core business to continue unhindered. The transition was so smooth that there was no market speculation, no public feuds—just a well-orchestrated, dignified handover.

The Legacy of a Well-Planned Transition

Today, the Munjal family stands as a testament to how foresight, professionalism, and unity can create enduring success across generations. Unlike the messy, headline-grabbing feuds of the Ambanis or the Raymond Group,

Hero's transition was built on strong governance, respect for elders, and an unwavering commitment to core values.

As I reflect on their journey, it's clear—leadership transitions are not just about passing the baton. They are about building systems that outlive individuals, nurturing a culture of trust, and having the humility to embrace change. Hero's story is a powerful lesson in how family businesses can thrive across generations without falling into the trap of internal discord.

And if there's one takeaway for aspiring business leaders, it's this—legacy isn't built on inheritance alone. It's built on wisdom, discipline, and the ability to adapt.

Bajaj Group

After discussing the remarkable leadership transition at the Hero Group, another example that comes to my mind is the Bajaj Group. Unlike many family-run businesses that falter under the weight of succession disputes, Rahul Bajaj orchestrated one of the most seamless and methodically planned transitions in India's corporate landscape. His foresight, discipline, and strategic thinking ensured that the Bajaj legacy not only remained intact but thrived across multiple industries.

Rahul Bajaj built the Bajaj Group into an industrial powerhouse, with two major verticals—Bajaj Auto, the company that once made scooters a household staple, and Bajaj Finserv, a financial behemoth. However, the true mark of his leadership was not just in building an empire but in how he transitioned it to the next generation without turmoil. When the time came to pass the torch, he divided the business between his two sons, Rajiv Bajaj and Sanjiv Bajaj, in a way that played to their strengths while maintaining the group's long-term sustainability.

Rajiv was entrusted with Bajaj Auto and steadily rose to become the Managing Director and later CEO, transforming the company into a global leader in motorcycles. Sanjiv, on the other hand, took charge of Bajaj Finserv, steering it into becoming one of India's most formidable financial services conglomerates.

1. **Preparing Children Professionally—Beyond Just a Surname**

Rahul Bajaj's approach was not about simply handing over the reins to his sons because they were family; he ensured they earned their leadership through education, rigorous training, and hands-on experience. He believed in preparing them professionally before entrusting them with significant responsibilities. This long-term grooming ensured that they were not just heirs but competent leaders who understood the business inside out.

Rajiv Bajaj's transformation of Bajaj Auto is a testament to this strategic foresight. He led the company's shift from being a scooter manufacturer to a dominant player in motorcycles, particularly in global markets. Meanwhile, Sanjiv Bajaj turned Bajaj Finserv into a financial powerhouse, revolutionizing how Indians approached lending, insurance, and investments, particularly in microfinance. Their success was not just about inheritance—it was about capability, preparation, and execution.

2. **Strong Corporate Governance and Mentoring—The Pillars of Stability**

Just as Brijmohan Lall Munjal relied on corporate governance to ensure a smooth transition, Rahul Bajaj employed similar principles. He didn't step away immediately after handing over the businesses. Instead, he remained the Chairman of the Bajaj Group until 2021, offering guidance, monitoring growth, and ensuring professionalism was upheld in both companies.

This allowed Rajiv and Sanjiv ample time to establish themselves as strong, independent leaders without internal conflicts overshadowing their progress.

By maintaining good governance and mentoring his sons even after they took the helm, he ensured that the transition was not just smooth but also built for long-term success.

3. Early Integration of Professionals at the Top Level

One of Rahul Bajaj's most significant moves was integrating top-tier professionals into leadership roles while keeping the strategic vision within the family. He ensured that the daily operations of both Bajaj Auto and Bajaj Finserv were managed by highly skilled professionals, allowing his sons to focus on larger business strategies rather than getting entangled in operational details.

This decision created a structured, professional approach to business management, reducing dependency on family members while still preserving the Bajaj legacy. It also minimized potential conflicts, as power was distributed efficiently rather than concentrated in a single entity.

4. Passing on the Legacy—Training the Next Generations

Rahul Bajaj believed that a legacy is not merely inherited; it is cultivated. Throughout his tenure, he remained actively involved in mentoring both his sons and the broader leadership team. He regularly attended meetings, provided strategic input, and instilled a strong value system that ensured both companies continued on the path of ethical and sustainable growth.

As a result, both Bajaj Auto and Bajaj Finserv are today considered jewels in India's corporate world, each thriving under its respective leader without any of the family disputes that have plagued other business dynasties. This is not just a story of leadership transition—it is a case study in succession planning done right.

The transitions at the Hero Group and the Bajaj Group provide invaluable lessons for businesses worldwide. While both had different styles, the core principles remained the same—early preparation, professional governance, strategic division of responsibilities, and an unwavering commitment to values.

In an era where business legacies are often tainted by succession battles, these stories stand out as beacons of wisdom. They remind us that true leadership is not just about building an empire—it's about ensuring that empire stands tall long after its founder steps away.

Like Mr. Brijmohan Lall Munjal, who deftly navigated the complexities of both family and business, the challenge always lies in drawing a clear line between personal and professional spheres.

One of the biggest hurdles in family-run businesses is ensuring that the second generation understands the discipline and struggle that went into building the empire they inherit. The founders—those who laid the foundation—knew what it was like to fight for every rupee, to work tirelessly without guarantees, and to make sacrifices for long-term success. But when the next generation enters the picture, they do so in an entirely different landscape. Unlike their predecessors, they don't start with empty pockets or sleepless nights wondering how to pay the next month's wages.

Instead, they arrive in a world of established wealth. They've traveled first-class, studied in prestigious institutions abroad, stayed in five-star hotels, and vacationed in exotic destinations—all without ever having to think twice. The struggle that defined the first generation is completely foreign to them. And then, as they settle into their roles, a new layer of complexity emerges—marriage. Their spouses, coming from equally privileged backgrounds, may or may not understand the sacrifices and discipline that built the business.

Suddenly, discussions revolve around extravagant purchases, social gatherings, and a lifestyle that feels like an entitlement rather than an earned reward.

This is where many businesses falter. The absence of financial discipline, combined with the ease of access to wealth, creates a dangerous complacency. Especially in businesses where cash flow is generated off the books, it becomes difficult to enforce boundaries.

If a company makes 20 lakh rupees in cash every month, how do you convince the next generation that the money isn't theirs to spend freely? They see it, they know it exists, and they expect a share. And once you start giving in—whether it's five lakhs or ten lakhs—it disappears into luxury spending: designer clothes, expensive watches, lavish parties. Financial discipline erodes, and with it, the values that built the business. For me, setting clear boundaries was non-negotiable. The first and most important rule? No unaccounted cash. Everything was structured. Everyone, including myself, was on a fixed salary. No matter how much the business made, we lived within our means. If my son wanted a lifestyle upgrade—a destination wedding anniversary in Turkey, for instance—he was more than welcome to do it. But on his salary, not the company's dime.

He would protest: "But I can't afford it with my salary."

And my answer was always the same: "Then you can't afford it."

The company's money was for business, not personal indulgences. No falsified bills, no creative accounting. This discipline, this governance, ensured that we never fell into the trap that so many successful businesses do—where personal luxuries bleed into professional finances.

Drawing these boundaries is critical. When you instill financial discipline and corporate governance from the outset, 80% of business problems simply disappear.

It's not just about business success; it's about building a legacy that lasts beyond one generation.

9

Giving Back

"Business as usual is no longer acceptable. The world needs businesses that care."

— Paul Polman

So far, I have talked about the patience it takes to build something meaningful, the role of integrity and honesty in sustaining it, and the importance of succession and legacy in ensuring that it lasts. But now, let's get to the real stuff—what it means to live these lessons.

I didn't set out to be an entrepreneur. In fact, business was never part of the conversation in our middle-class, academically inclined households. Success, in the traditional sense, was always linked to education, stability, and service—not enterprise. But as I grew, I realized that entrepreneurship, when built on the right values, could be a powerful tool—not just for creating wealth but for redistributing it meaningfully.

Success isn't just about what we build—it's about what we leave behind. The real legacy of an entrepreneur isn't measured in profits alone but in the impact they have on the people and communities around them.

Entrepreneurship doesn't end at just strategy and execution; it's about impact. The true measure of success isn't found in balance sheets or market dominance but in the lives we touch, the communities we uplift, and the legacy we leave behind. Wealth, when used with purpose, becomes a force for good. Giving back turns into more than just a responsibility—it's a privilege that transforms both the giver and the world around them.

For many, philanthropy isn't an occasional gesture, an afterthought, or a public relations exercise—but a way of life. The Sikh tenet of *Dasvandh*—the practice of setting aside 10% of one's earnings for the greater good—illustrates this beautifully. It's not about obligation; it's about belief. The belief that success is meant to be shared, that no one rises alone, and that true wealth is measured by

how many lives we uplift. This belief has powered centuries of community-driven initiatives, funding free meals, education, and healthcare through Gurudwaras and beyond.

Many successful businesses follow the same path, not because they have to, but because they understand that true success is shared. They build schools, fund hospitals, create jobs, and reinvest in the communities that shaped them. Over time, these acts of giving do more than just provide aid—they build trust, forge lasting legacies, and remind us that real wealth isn't measured by what we accumulate but by what we give away.

The Chief Minister of Haryana, Bhupinder Singh Hooda inaugurating our De-addiction Center in Faridabad.

In the end, success isn't about how high we climb—it's about how many we lift along the way.

Growing up, I was fortunate enough to have this sense of philanthropy inculcated in me by witnessing it firsthand. My grandfather, a respected lawyer in Punjab, made it a point to support the education of children from underprivileged backgrounds, such as the local rickshaw-wala's kids and the local help. He never sought recognition—he simply believed in doing the right thing. Although a college professor with a reasonable income, my father would hold free evening classes to train his students for the Indian Administrative Services (IAS) and Indian Revenue Services (IRS) exams, many of whom later became distinguished officers. My mother, too, quietly played her part, ensuring the children of laborers and rickshaw pullers received an education. Giving wasn't a grand gesture; it was woven into the fabric of everyday life.

So, when I started my own business, success was never just about financial growth. The lessons from my family shaped my approach—I looked for ways to support the people I met along the way, whether through mentorship, financial assistance, or simply creating opportunities for those who needed them. My wife shared the same values, and together, we found fulfillment in making a difference, no matter how small.

Over the years, I've seen how deeply philanthropy is tied to entrepreneurship. Many of the most respected business leaders I know don't just create wealth; they create value. They build schools, hospitals, and infrastructure, not because they have to, but because they want to. In small towns across India, successful entrepreneurs have long upheld the tradition of constructing *Dharamshalas*—community spaces used for marriages, religious gatherings, and shelter for travelers—long before luxury hotels existed.

This move has had a profound impact, channeling business success into tangible societal benefits, from education and healthcare to environmental sustainability. This wasn't just a policy shift—it was a philosophical milestone. It formalized what many already believed: that wealth, when combined with intent, can transform lives.

But beyond policy and tradition, the true essence of philanthropy in entrepreneurship lies in intention. Some see it as a responsibility, others as a privilege—but in the end, it's about values. It's about understanding that wealth is most meaningful when it's used to create opportunities for others. It's about realizing that success, at its core, is a shared journey.

Perhaps it's about something even deeper—the unshakable belief that when we uplift others, we elevate ourselves.

For today's entrepreneur, I believe the philanthropic mindset is a hybrid—it's both a duty and a privilege. It's a responsibility because success should not exist in a vacuum; it must ripple *outward*. And it's a privilege because we are in a position to create that ripple. True philanthropy, when practiced through the lens of entrepreneurship, is not mere charity. It's a strategic, long-term investment in the kind of society we want to help build.

Ultimately, how one gives back reveals as much about their values as how they build their business. That, to me, is the real legacy of entrepreneurship. As our business grew and earned recognition, so did our desire to give back meaningfully. Two initiatives, in particular, are very close to my heart—not just because of their scale but because of the lives they've touched.

The first is a De-Addiction and Mental Health Centre in Faridabad. While living in the city, I became actively involved with the Faridabad Industries Association, a strong and respected voice in Haryana's industrial landscape. During my tenure, I rose to the position of President of Faridabad Industry Association (FIA), and it became increasingly clear to us that substance abuse was a growing menace—especially among factory workers and youth.

Given our company's expertise in pharmaceuticals, we conceived a center dedicated to de-addiction and mental health.

We collaborated with expert psychiatrists and clinical psychologists, established a facility, and ensured that all essential medications were provided free of cost by our company. We charged only a nominal fee to ensure serious participation. Today, the center supports 10 - 15 patients daily in the OPD and houses 15–20 patients at any given time. We offer not just medical support but holistic care—yoga, counselling, and long-term mental health solutions. The center has been running successfully for the last 10 years, and to me, it remains one of our most impactful contributions to society.

The second initiative is a deeply personal tribute: the Shri Vishwanath and Vimal Chawla Medical Centre, built in memory of my parents in a local Arya Samaj Mandir in Sector 15, Faridabad. Seeing how stroke affects so many families—including my friends' parents—I envisioned a physiotherapy and rehabilitation center exclusively for stroke patients.

6th September, 2019, I was honored with a "Lifetime Achievement Award" by the Faridabad Industry Association, a 60-year-old industry association representing medium to large industries.

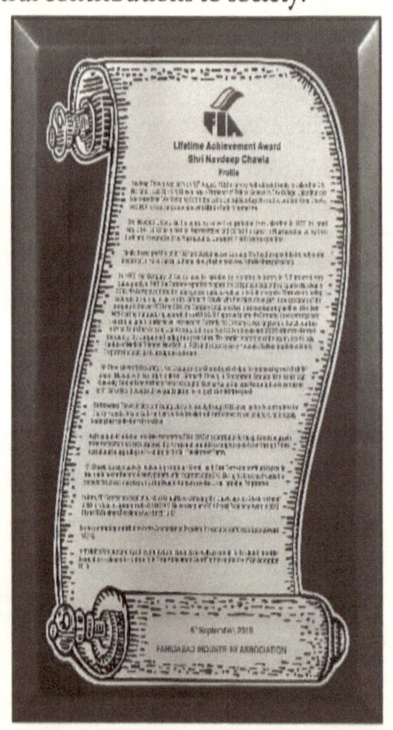

Picture of LifeTime Achievement Award conferred on me by Faridabad Industry Association

On 20th October, 2023, I was conferred the Degree of "Doctor of Philosophy (PhD) HONORIS CAUSA" for my service to the Pharmaceutical Industry Society and giving back to society.

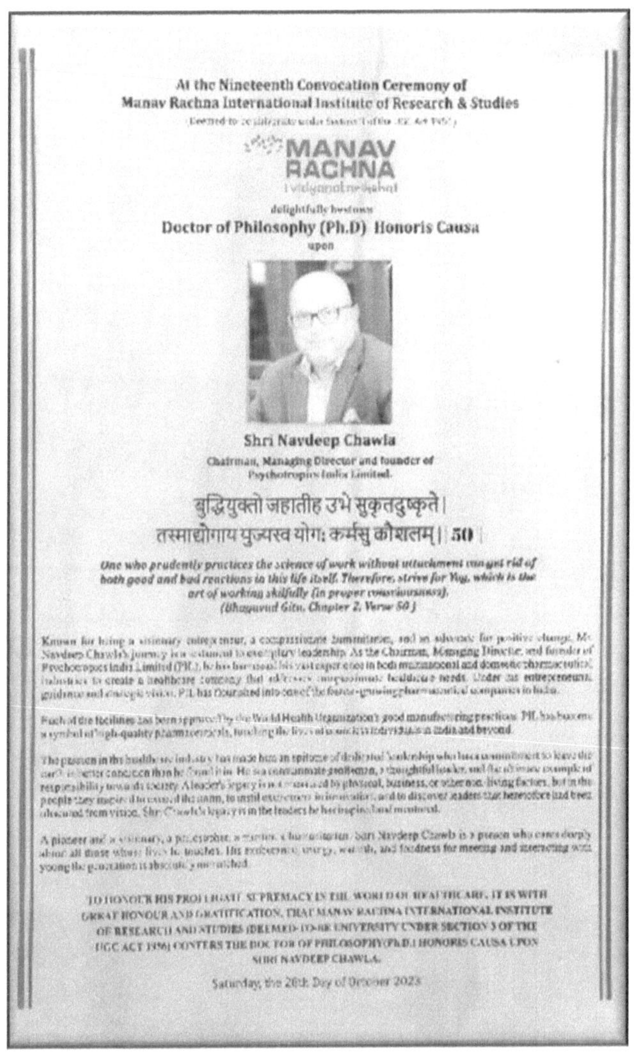

Award of Honorary PhD conferred by a reputed Manav Rachna International Institute of Research & Studies University
(Deemed to be university under section 3 of the UGC Act 1956)

With support from Rotary International, we constructed a modern facility in collaboration with Manav Rachna University's College of Physiotherapy.

Their postgraduate students intern here, and in complex cases, faculty members step in to ensure high-quality treatment. The physiotherapy center alone sees 20+ patients daily, while the ground

Rotary Cancer Detection Bus

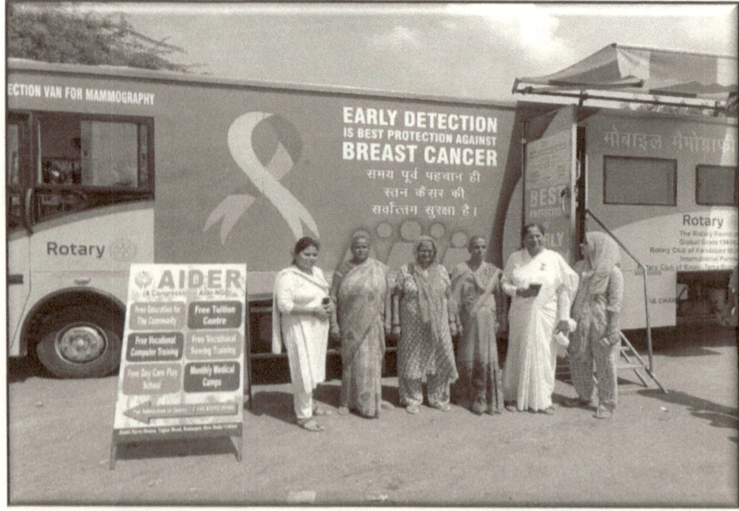

Initiative of FLA Charitable Society in collaboration with Rotary Club to send bus equipped with all equipment's for early detection of breast cancer

floor also houses dental, Ayurvedic, and general OPDs, all supported by university experts. Our company continues to supply free medications for all patients here.

Beyond these two flagship initiatives, our CSR efforts extend to:

- Rotary Blood Bank for Thalassemia patients: We set up a Rotary Blood Bank with the help of industry colleagues, specifically to assist children with thalassemia who need blood transfusions and medication every month. Many of these children come from families earning as little as ₹15,000 per month—how can they spend ₹8,000 per month on treatment? Our initiative now supports over 200 children, not only from Faridabad but also from Ghaziabad, Delhi, and surrounding towns. Families have even relocated closer to our center so their children can receive proper care. We ensure safe, high-quality blood—collected only from healthy donors within our industry ecosystem, not from commercial donors. This is our way of standing in for families in their most vulnerable moments.
- Cancer detection camps through a mobile mammography unit
- Cervical cancer vaccination programs for young girls
- Donation of over $500,000 to the Rotary Foundation, with a personal commitment to support new projects every year.

The Rotary matches these donations to create a sustainable impact in healthcare, education, water management, and the environment. Being part of Rotary's Arch Klumph Society Trustee Circle (AKS)—where fewer than 300 members exist worldwide at my level—has been a humbling honor. Our photo is etched in glass at their Evanston headquarters, a symbol not of wealth, but of shared purpose.

A health Center built and being operated in the memory of my parents in Arya Samaj Sector-15, Faridabad

Additionally, due to our contribution of $5,00,000 to the Rotary Foundation, we were invited to the Rotary International Headquarters in Evanston, USA, and our glass portrait was placed in the Rotary Gallery among the few donors worldwide.

*Our Glass Portrait has been placed in the Rotary International Headquarters,
in Evanston, USA*

We also regularly provide free essential medicines—including anti-diabetic, antihypertensive, and antibiotic drugs—to charitable institutions, temples, and senior citizen homes serving thousands across the year.

Doctors from these institutions send us a list of required medicines from our catalog, and our office ensures that these needs are fulfilled regularly and free of cost.

My wife, too, has dedicated herself to social causes. She supports an orphanage for girls—funding their education, helping them secure jobs through the Faridabad Industries network, and even arranging their marriages with dignity and care. These girls are equipped with not just degrees, but also the emotional and material support to begin life on their own terms.

She is also deeply involved in arranging weddings for visually impaired couples, having supported over 100 such marriages in recent years. Each couple is provided with household essentials and a sense of family they may not have had otherwise. These acts of giving have brought us immense respect—not because we sought it, but because people recognize sincerity. Many times, institutions have honored us publicly. But that was never the intention. As I often say, acquiring another asset or material possession pales in comparison to the joy of restoring dignity, health, or hope to someone's life.

One of the projects closest to my heart is our Mammography Bus—a fully-equipped mobile screening unit with all the necessary mammography equipment. This bus was handed over to our FIA charitable society for its smooth running and maintenance by the Rotary Club of Faridabad Midtown. The bus travels to rural areas, where awareness about breast cancer is still very limited and social stigma runs deep. In these regions, women are often too shy or uninformed to speak up, let alone get tested. By the time symptoms are visible, it's already the fourth stage. So we took it upon ourselves, through the support of Rotary Clubs and fellow industrialists, to bring the screening to them.

It costs ₹25,000 per trip to run the bus. We ask Rotary Clubs for a ₹5000 contribution, and sometimes local business owners generously step in to offer another ₹10,000 to help us subsidize the rest. Each trip sees about 25–30 women screened.

Out of every 1000 women, 1-2 are usually found to be at risk. If even one life is saved, the entire effort is worth it. We've tied up with a radiology company that provides digital reporting. The reports are handled confidentially by a radiology center through digital channels, so even their identity remains protected. Since anonymity is often a concern, the reports are handled with the utmost confidentiality. If there's a suspected case, they're contacted directly and guided toward the nearest center for further consultation. Even if two or three women out of one thousand are detected early, that's two or three lives possibly saved. And that, in itself, makes it worthwhile.

That bus—built at a cost of ₹1,00,00,000—carries more than just equipment. It carries hope, awareness, and the silent promise that someone is looking out for them. The bus continues to run only because of a collective industry vision and the help of people who see value in serving silently, without fanfare. When they see that we're able to manage all this alongside running a business, they begin to believe that it's possible.

We have also extended our hand beyond the healthcare field by actively supporting local sporting events—golf, athletics, and more—by sponsoring prizes and players and enabling the organizations that run these events. It's another way we connect with the community, promote health, and invest in young talent.

When people ask how we find time for all this while still growing as a business, I say—we take out just two hours a day to serve others, and the rest, I believe, is God's doing. That's what draws others to join us.

That's how collective action builds something far more powerful than individual success. And slowly, the others begin to join us, too.

That, truly, is the reward of philanthropy.

Integrating community service or philanthropy into a business model not only strengthens brand reputation and customer loyalty but also fosters long-term goodwill among employees, customers, and the community. The key lies in aligning CSR initiatives with your core values and operational strengths.

Let me share a few examples that demonstrate how this can be done effectively:

One remarkable example is DLF Group, a leading real estate company with a strong reputation for quality and community development. I have personally seen their philanthropic approach in action as a resident of one of their properties and a member of their prestigious golf club. Through their *DLF CARES* Program, they provide free education to the children of workers employed in their organization on a contractual basis, including academic counselling and career guidance for high-performing students. They also engage and employ youth with special needs across their condominiums—at clubhouses, spas, and service counters—sensitizing residents to treat them with dignity and patience. It's a beautiful example of inclusive employment that creates value for the community without burdening the business model.

Similarly, Bharti Airtel, a telecom giant, has invested significantly in rural education. They've established fully equipped higher secondary schools with modern infrastructure and quality teaching, exclusively for the children of contractual workers and other underserved families. These schools match urban standards but are run in remote areas, completely free of cost.

Their investment in education is building future-ready communities while enhancing their brand value across India.

In my own experience as Chairman of the Faridabad Industry Association (FIA) Charitable Society, we've integrated philanthropy into the very fabric of our industrial ecosystem. For instance, tree plantation is an ongoing initiative where we involve industries directly—we plant lakhs of trees each year and ask companies to maintain the ones planted near their premises. It's simple, sustainable, and has a measurable impact on the local environment.

Another impactful initiative was launched during the COVID-19 crisis. We identified 150 students who had lost one or both parents due to the pandemic. Through FIA, we supported their complete schooling, ensuring they could continue their education without financial burden. Over the past few years, nearly 100 of these children have completed their education, and we continue to support the rest until they can stand on their own feet.

The essence of successful philanthropy lies in creating long-term, structured initiatives that dovetail with your business ethos—whether it's in healthcare, education, environment, or inclusive employment. And contrary to the misconception, these initiatives don't have to compromise profitability. In fact, they enhance the emotional equity of a brand, build trust, and inspire a sense of purpose among all stakeholders.

Since the introduction of Section 135 of the Companies Act in 2014, the Government of India has played a pivotal role in institutionalizing Corporate Social Responsibility (CSR).

What's commendable is that this mandate hasn't been seen as a burden—it's been embraced as an opportunity by companies across the spectrum. In 2024 alone, over ₹1,00,000 crore was spent on CSR initiatives in India.

This massive wave of giving back reflects not just legal compliance but a growing culture of corporate compassion. Much of this can be credited to the visionary leadership of Prime Minister Modi, who introduced this idea in a way that encouraged participation rather than enforcement—inviting the private sector to become co-creators in national development. If we look at some standout companies, HDFC Bank has emerged as the highest spender, with ₹945 crore allocated to CSR last year. Reliance Industries follows closely with ₹900 crore, and Tata Consultancy Services (TCS) spent ₹827 crore. Then we have ONGC at ₹636 crore, Tata Steel with ₹580 crore, Indian Oil Corporation at ₹458 crore, Infosys at ₹456 crore, and ITC at ₹400 crore. These numbers are not just statistics—they represent tangible contributions to India's social fabric.

What other businesses can learn from these organizations is this: giving back doesn't weaken your brand—it strengthens it. It builds long-term trust, enhances your corporate image, and inspires loyalty from both customers and employees. It can even create meaningful partnerships with local communities, educational institutions, and NGOs, extending your business impact far beyond profit.

Even small and mid-sized enterprises (SMEs) earning above the ₹5 crore threshold are now stepping up. Many have begun integrating CSR into their operations not just to comply with regulations, but because they recognize the value of contributing meaningfully to the society in which they operate.

In today's business world, social responsibility is no longer optional. It's becoming a core part of brand identity—and the most successful companies are those that lead with purpose, not just profit.

You simply cannot run a CSR program in isolation. It's not something that can be done behind closed doors. It requires thoughtful planning and, most importantly, the wholehearted involvement of your people. When employees understand *why* you're doing something for the greater good, they don't just comply—they participate with pride. They begin to see the company not merely as an employer, but as an institution that cares.

This fosters a deep emotional connection and instills confidence: "If our company is helping others without being asked, it will surely support us if we ever need help."

This sentiment translates directly into loyalty, trust, and morale. In our case, this has contributed significantly to a strong, stable culture. We have one of the lowest attrition rates in the industry. I have team members who have been with us for 37–39 years. Imagine—when they started, their salaries were ₹5,000–6,000. Today, they earn ₹3–5 lakhs monthly and drive company vehicles.

That kind of continuity doesn't come from compensation alone—it comes from belief in the organization's values and the leader's integrity.

Philanthropy isn't just a side project for us—it's a part of who we are. And in return, it makes us stronger, more united, and more resilient as a business. The initiatives have strengthened our company culture in ways that are difficult to measure, but deeply felt. They've built trust within our teams and created a positive perception among our customers and the wider community

However, this journey is not without its own hurdles. Some of the biggest challenges don't come from within the organization—they come from outside. Over the years, I've seen how politicians and political interests interfere with genuine CSR work. Many of them float NGOs—not necessarily to serve the community but to support their own campaigns or constituency work. They don't want to spend from their own pockets, so they come knocking on the doors of businesses that are known to give.

And the problem isn't just the ask. The accountability is completely missing. Many of these NGOs don't provide proper utilization certificates. And even if they do, you're often left questioning the authenticity of those documents.

In our own charity organization, we make sure everything is accounted for—every rupee spent is supported by photos, documentation, and a proper paper trail. That's how we believe it should be done.

But the pressure is real. Once people know that someone like Navdeep Chawla donates to and supports various causes, the calls start coming. "He helped with opening a blood bank, a health center—he'll surely give something to us too." And sometimes, just to avoid unnecessary trouble, we end up giving even when we don't feel good about it. It's a difficult space to navigate in a society where your goodwill can also be exploited.

Looking back at our own journey, it's a story of small beginnings. We didn't start out as a large corporation—we built ourselves up over the years. And as we grew, we made a conscious decision to give back. Whether it was distributing free medicines to charitable institutions in our town, or focusing on thalassemia patients who need blood and expensive medicines every single month, we kept asking ourselves: *How can we help?*

We didn't wait to become a "big business" before doing good. Even when we had limited resources, we started supporting causes we believed in. These aren't big gestures—they're consistent ones. That, to me, is what entrepreneurship-driven philanthropy really means.

You know, philanthropy wasn't something I stumbled upon later in life. Right from the beginning, I told myself—*If ever in life I get the strength, the means, or the position to help others, I will give back to society.* I think that intention—that prayer—reached the right ears.

God was kind, and as we grew, we found both the opportunity and the people to support.

And yes, meeting the beneficiaries of our work changed me.

There's a father who travels two hours each way every day for work, just so he can stay close to our center, where his thalassemic child gets free treatment. Imagine that. They moved homes—not for a better job or house—but because they found a place that would help their child survive. That touches you deeply.

We never wanted to be known for big degrees or flashy credentials. I'm not someone with a double MBA or foreign education.

I just completed my graduation, worked 8 to 10 hours a day, sometimes even 12 to 16 hours, stayed honest, and tried to build something meaningful—with a clean mind and good intentions. If our journey, in any way, can be considered inspiring, then I genuinely believe it's because we kept our hearts in the right place.

I always tell people—*don't wait for the "right time" or a huge surplus to start giving.* Just start, however small. You don't need crores to make a difference. What you need is intent and the courage to act on it.

When we run NGOs or charitable projects through industry associations, we often appeal to businesses based on their size or turnover. Suppose someone's turnover is ₹400 crore—we might request ₹1–2 lakhs for a good cause. But you'll be surprised how many of them don't take it seriously.

Still, I don't hold it against them. I've learnt that if someone says no or gives an unconvincing answer, I simply never ask them again. Not because I'm angry—but because I feel maybe they're not ready yet. Maybe God hasn't yet given them the clarity or courage to think beyond personal wealth. Because let's face it—how much do we need, really? You earn, you buy a few flats—one in Bombay, one in Goa, ten plots here and there... and then what? Life is short. After 80, we all leave it behind. And I've seen this with my own eyes—what follows is family fighting over who gets what, and at what value.

Is this what we work for?

Whenever I speak at functions hosted by our charitable society, I speak openly—no marketing, no preaching. I simply tell them that *not doing charity is a debt, and doing it is a blessing.* I believe when you do good with a clean heart, God keeps your path clear. I've seen that when you speak from the heart, people listen. Out of 100 entrepreneurs in the audience, at least 4–5 come forward every time to ask, *"How can I help?"* You don't need to push or convince people. Just show them a living example. Continue doing good work, and eventually, they'll realize—*this is the path God has made for us, and we must follow it.*

Looking back, I feel deeply grateful—not just for what I've received in life, but for the opportunity to give back. Philanthropy is not something I stumbled into late in life. It was always a part of my belief system—that if God ever gave me the strength and means, I would use it to serve society.

Through years of hard work, honest dealings, and the support of countless people—from loyal employees to generous well-wishers— we were able to create something larger than just a successful business. We created impact. Real, tangible, soul-touching impact.

Whether it's providing free medicines, supporting children with thalassemia, enabling access to clean blood, physiotherapy for stroke patients, or sponsoring young athletes—we never looked at these as "CSR projects." They were simply the right thing to do. And when you do the right thing consistently, people join you. Employees take pride in their work. Customers respect you more.

Even competitors quietly appreciate what you stand for.

My advice to others is simple: Start small. Start with whatever you have. But start. The world doesn't need only billionaires to bring change. It needs good-hearted people willing to do what they can.

You don't need a foreign degree or fancy credentials. Just the will to serve, the honesty to stay grounded, and the wisdom to know when to let go of what you don't need.

In the end, the joy of giving is unmatched. It brings peace, purpose, and a sense of connection to something greater than yourself. And if I could walk this path and find fulfilment, so can you.

Let your business be your blessing—and let your blessings be shared.

10

The Long Road to Balance

"Leadership is not about being in charge. It is about taking care of those in your charge."

— Simon Sinek

In the beginning, there was no talk of balance—only survival. For many self-made entrepreneurs, the idea of "work-life balance" is a luxury that arrives much later—if at all. In the early stages, when you're transitioning from the security of a job to the uncertainty of running your own venture, balance isn't even part of the vocabulary. The priority is survival, not serenity.

Most entrepreneurs start with minimal capital, immense ambition, and no room for failure. The mindset is clear: "I cannot afford to lose." Every decision is infused with urgency, and every setback is treated as a lesson rather than a deterrent. There's little time—or emotional space—to ponder boundaries between work and personal life. You're all in. The only way out is through.

When I stepped away from the comfort of a salaried job and into the unpredictable world of entrepreneurship, the idea of "work-life balance" felt quite distant, almost laughable.

I started with very little—meager capital, a handful of lessons from my past roles, and an unwavering determination not to fail. When failure isn't an option, you don't think about work-life balance. You think about how to keep the lights on. How to make the next sale. How to prove to yourself that this leap wasn't a mistake.

Every single day was a test. There was no backup plan. No guidebook. Just instinct, relentless work, and a quiet voice inside saying, "Keep going." When two packing boys didn't show up at the factory, I sat down and packed the goods myself. If something had to be delivered and no one was available, I strapped it to the back of my motorcycle and rode it to the transporter.

These weren't exceptions—they were the rule. Sixteen-hour days weren't considered "long"; they were just... normal. Lunch happened when there was time. Tea breaks didn't exist.

There were no boundaries between personal and professional life—just a single, unbroken line of effort, from morning till midnight.

In these foundational years, you learn by doing. There's no handbook, no mentor always at hand. You rely on your past job experience, quickly adapting, absorbing, and evolving. It's a crucible of growth—and balance simply doesn't feature in that equation.

Eventually, though, things begin to shift. After a decade or two of relentless hustle, success starts to take shape. That's when entrepreneurs begin to reflect: *Should I be spending more time with family? Can I delegate more? Is it time to reclaim my weekends?*

But getting to that point requires navigating a journey marked by a few key principles:

1. **Calculated Risk and Relentless Forward Motion:** When failure isn't an option, the focus sharpens. You plan meticulously, strategize continuously, and push forward with unflinching commitment. Every early win fuels confidence and opens doors—building momentum that becomes its own motivator.

2. **Ethics, Hard Work, and Staying the Course:** The entrepreneurial world is filled with temptations—shortcuts that promise faster results. But in the long run, those who stay ethical, persistent, and grounded create businesses with strong foundations. They build trust—not just with customers but with their teams and themselves.

3. **Innovation as a Differentiator:** Startups that survive and thrive often offer something new—whether it's in their product, service, or delivery model. Innovation doesn't have to be flashy; it just needs to be *valuable*. Creating value for every rupee your customer spends builds loyalty and lowers the risk of failure.

4. **Reinvesting Wisely and Running Lean:** Early profits are tempting. Many entrepreneurs splurge—upgrading their lifestyles prematurely. But those who reinvest, scale cautiously, and maintain lean operations set themselves up for long-term sustainability. Every team member must become a multi-tasker; every rupee must stretch.

In the early years, there was no such thing as 'office hours.' You work until the job is done. Whether it's packing goods yourself when labor doesn't show up, or delivering them personally on your motorcycle, the entrepreneur wears every hat—often at once.

Only much later—when the business is stable, operations are delegated, and trust is built—you gain the *luxury* of routine.

Then, and only then, does work-life balance become a consideration: fixed lunch breaks, golf on weekends, time with family. Until then, it's grit, grind, and growth.

"Balance is earned—not at the beginning of the journey,
but through it."

This lived experience isn't a deterrent; it's a truth with which many entrepreneurs resonate deeply. Understanding it is the first step to eventually creating boundaries—not just as a personal privilege but as a strategic business necessity.

The Fire That Didn't Burn Out

When people speak about burnout in business, they often speak of thresholds—crossing over from ambition to exhaustion, from determination to depletion. But what if you never cross that line? What if the fire simply keeps burning, steady and bright, without ever scorching the spirit? That's how it was for me. I didn't experience burnout. Not because I was superhuman, not because I had some secret formula, but because of the way I approached the work—and perhaps, more importantly, the way I approached people.

At the age of 31, I set out to build my own business. I don't think we wholly understood what burnout was. And when you're young and gushing adrenaline, the word 'burnout' misses making it to our vocabulary. It was just work—and I loved it. There was an energy in those early days that carried me from 8 in the morning to, sometimes, 12 at night, with barely a break in between. And when the official work was done, the unofficial part would begin. Entertaining customers, hosting dinners at home, or taking them out—this was not a chore. It was part of the job, yes, but it also brought me joy.

And something magical happened over time. These transactional relationships deepened. Customers became friends. Friends became family. The boundary between personal and professional blurred into something richer—something warmer. Our homes became shared spaces of celebration and connection. We'd talk about everything—from pricing and delivery timelines to our children's milestones and family weddings. There was an emotional equity that grew alongside the business.

That's the secret no one tells you: When your work is laced with purpose and your relationships are grounded in trust, fatigue doesn't stand a chance. There were long hours and high stakes, but never any warning signs. No need for recovery. The goal was clear: to succeed—and to succeed quickly. That singular, unshakeable focus became my prayer, my fuel.

Far from being a source of burnout, they became my respite, my way of unwinding. In retrospect, perhaps that's why I never spotted any warning signs. There was no recovery plan in place because I never fell into the pit of overwork. There was prayer, there was clarity, and there was the stubborn commitment to grow — quickly, steadily, and meaningfully.

But let me be clear — even without burnout, the road was not without its burdens.

Wearing All the Hats—And Loving It

Time management is a strange phrase in the early stages of business. You don't manage time—you squeeze it, stretch it, bargain with it. Every minute has to work for you. The challenges are familiar to anyone who has ever started from scratch: limited resources, cutthroat competition, the relentless push to produce more at lower costs, and the perpetual demand to do it all faster and better.

So, what do you do? You become everyone. Every day becomes a juggling act. You're the production manager, ensuring delivery timelines are met. You're the HR head, cultivating loyalty and morale in your lean team. You're the product development lead, scouring markets for trends, innovating or sourcing new products with barely any prior experience.

You're the marketer, the quality inspector, the customer care rep, the tea-maker if need be.

But here's what makes it sustainable: you build systems—not necessarily digital ones, at least not at first—but human ones. You train your people to think like owners. You share the vision, not just the tasks. You invest time not just in running the business but in teaching others how to run it alongside you.

I didn't use a fancy planner or an app. My time management tool was awareness of what mattered most, of who needed me, and of how to say no when required. I chose progress over perfection. And gradually, my role began to shift from doing everything myself to ensuring everything was being done by the right people, at the right time.

Delegation wasn't an option initially, as there was no one to delegate to. The challenge was not just working hard — it was working smart under constraints. We had to build something substantial while running lean.

And yet, this phase was crucial. It taught me everything I needed to know about how businesses are run — not from boardrooms, but from factory floors, sales calls, and tough client meetings. I also learned to listen — to employees, to customers, and to mentors — absorbing insights that no textbook could provide. Those conversations shaped my instincts, helped refine my judgment, and kept me grounded.

The Art of Letting Go (But Not Really)

As we tasted success, the real challenge wasn't just scaling — it was letting go. I learnt early on that if you want to grow, you have to let go. But not recklessly. Delegation isn't just about assigning tasks. It's about designing trust. That only happens when you've identified capable people, trained them well, and given them not just responsibility but ownership as well.

Delegation had to replace micromanagement. That shift wasn't easy. When you've built something from scratch, trusting others with it feels like handing over your child. But it was necessary.

As our business grew, delegation became the only way to keep up. It started small—getting someone else to handle routine calls, then overseeing deliveries, and eventually managing entire departments. But it only worked because I made it work. I set deadlines. I measured outcomes.

I rewarded good performance consistently. It was not micromanagement. It was care.

We began by identifying people who showed promise — not necessarily those with the best degrees, but those with a hunger to learn. Training became non-negotiable. Roles were defined, deadlines were established, and rewards were given for success. That's how we created a team we could trust. One hire led to another, and slowly, departments took shape. It felt like watching the skeletal framework of a dream come to life with muscle and movement.

Standard Operating Procedures (SOPs) were introduced. Consultants came in to set benchmarks. We fostered a learning culture — not just within the organization, but also by sending our people to seminars, workshops, and training events. The message was clear: we're in this together, and everyone has a stake in our collective success.

Then came automation. This was not some grand digital transformation with consultants and big budgets. It was pragmatic. Step-by-step. From handwritten ledgers to cloud-based accounting, from manual HR to digital payroll systems — we invested in tools that brought efficiency, reduced errors, and helped us scale. Software for CRM, project management, digital marketing, and production planning didn't just improve processes — they gave us insights. Real-time data meant real-time decisions. Lean systems for lean teams. It transformed how we thought about operations — not as a series of tasks, but as a dynamic, interlinked ecosystem.

I often tell younger entrepreneurs: if your accountant still writes ledgers by hand, you're not running a business, you're babysitting a time bomb. Automation isn't optional—it's essential. It reduces errors, saves time, and allows you to focus on growth, not grunt work.

Adapting When the Ground Shifts

The thing about business is—it changes. Sometimes slowly, sometimes overnight. You either adapt or you disappear. I've faced my share of curveballs, but I've come to see them as recalibrations, not catastrophes.

Resilience, I've learned, is non-negotiable. You cannot lead if you panic at the first sign of trouble. When COVID-19 hit, businesses around us crumbled. Ours didn't. Not because we were immune, but because we were ready. For years, we had resisted the temptation to splurge. No luxury cars on EMIs. No flamboyant offices. No bloated teams. We reinvested our profits or saved them. That foresight became our safety net. This isn't about frugality. It's about discipline. I've seen young entrepreneurs confuse revenue with wealth. One good year, and they're spending like royalty—branded gear, imported watches, swanky rentals.

From the outside, they appear to be success stories. But inside, they're one disruption away from collapse.

That's the other thing about today's business landscape—it moves faster than ever. Product relevance is fleeting. A friend once told me his family had sold the same 'Hing' (asafoetida) for fifty years without changing the formula. That era is over. Today, if your product lasts five years, you're lucky. You have to pivot constantly—sometimes even before the market signals it.

That's why we built adaptability into our DNA. We encouraged initiative, welcomed bold ideas, and trained our team to lead. We created systems that didn't collapse when I stepped away. Making yourself dispensable isn't a threat to your authority—it's the greatest gift you can give your business.

To keep pace, we invested in R&D. We travelled, spotted trends, and reimagined them for our market. A product discovered in a London pharmacy might spark a bestseller in India. We didn't copy. We adapted, tested, and refined our approach. Pilot batches, honest feedback, constant iteration—that became our method.

And data became our compass. Not just numbers, but insights. Trends. Risks. Opportunities. Monthly analytics became a ritual. We could predict seasonal surges, spot dips early, and innovate ahead of the curve. That agility—that mindset—is what kept us not just afloat, but ahead.

A Steady Flame

People wait for the burnout to come, like it's some rite of passage. And if it doesn't, they feel guilty or assume they're not working hard enough. But maybe the goal isn't to burn and rise again like a phoenix. Maybe the goal is to glow—consistently, sustainably, and with purpose.

I didn't burn out because I didn't chase the high of hustle. I built for the long run. I found joy in the journey. I surrounded myself with people who gave me energy, not took it away. And most of all, I stayed true to the one simple goal: to build something that would last longer than me.

Success wasn't the fire. It was the steady flame we kept alive—day after day, year after year.

Every entrepreneur has failures. Ours weren't always visible. Sometimes, we launched products that didn't perform as expected. Initially, I blamed the product. But later, I realized the flaw was in communication. My team wasn't equipped to explain the product's value. So we didn't scrap the product — we invested in training. The realization that execution gaps were often people gaps — that was a game-changer.

Speed is everything now. The market is unforgiving. 'Slow and steady' is a myth of the past. Agility, adaptability, and accountability are the cornerstones of the modern business landscape. So, we've trained our team to move fast — to spot errors early, pivot quickly, and stay alert. Failure isn't shameful anymore — inertia is. We created a 'Red Alert' internal system — any employee can raise a flag about a potential issue. This created psychological safety and built a culture of accountability.

When you play the long game, nothing matters more than ethical leadership. Companies like Tata, Infosys, HDFC, Hero — they've all demonstrated that success built on strong ethics lasts longer and means more. In contrast, companies like Satyam or Kingfisher remind us how quickly unethical decisions can bring down empires.

We built our company on trust. That's not a PR slogan — it's a business strategy. Our clients trust us with sensitive projects. Our team trusts us with their careers. Our vendors trust us to pay on time.

That ecosystem of trust is our most valuable asset. And we protect it fiercely. Transparency is embedded in our processes. We disclose when things go wrong. We apologise when we're late. And we over-communicate during crises. Even in hiring, we look for integrity as much as skill. One dishonest employee can undo the work of a hundred loyal ones. We've learned that lesson the hard way.

The Second Act: Balance and Legacy

After three decades in business, something shifts. You start to think about life differently. Your children begin to take the reins. You reflect more. Plan more. Live a little slower.

Work-life balance doesn't come early in this line of work. You earn it. You build towards it. And when you finally get there, it's a beautiful place. You have wealth, but you also have wisdom. You can now give back to your team, to your community, to your family. You spend weekends with your spouse, share business insights with your children, and perhaps mentor a budding entrepreneur now and then.

And yet, challenges remain. You want to reconnect with old friends — some of whom may not have been as fortunate. How do you invite them into your world without making them feel uncomfortable? Can you gift them something without making them feel indebted? These are the delicate questions of a life well-lived. Of success tempered with empathy.

Now, I no longer measure my worth by quarterly growth. I look at how many people I've helped rise. How many lives I've improved. How many relationships I've nurtured. How many lessons I've passed on. This is what coming full circle feels like. It's not about the bottom line anymore. It's about legacy. About being remembered not just as a successful entrepreneur, but as a good human being.

And that, perhaps, is the true goal of any entrepreneurial journey.

The Burn and the Build

Looking back, I realize the journey was never about achieving perfect balance.

The entrepreneurship journey is rarely linear, and even less often is it balanced from the outset. But balance, as I've come to understand, isn't something you inherit—it's something you cultivate. It's earned in the trenches of uncertainty, sharpened through years of trial, and refined by an evolving understanding of what really matters. Initially, the scale is heavily tipped towards survival. Yet over time, with conscious effort and courageous letting go, it begins to even out.

To reach that point, an entrepreneur must first embrace the chaos. You must be everything, do everything, and hold it all together with vision and sweat. But in doing so, you learn. You learn what your business truly needs. You learn where your energy is best spent. And you learn that success is not just about growth metrics, but about creating something that can eventually function—even flourish—without your constant presence.

What keeps you from burning out is not superhuman stamina. It's clarity of purpose, emotional investment in people, and the humility to delegate when the time is right. When relationships are genuine and the work aligns with your values, it doesn't deplete you—it energizes you. That's the paradox. The very thing that looks exhausting from the outside can be deeply fulfilling when it's built on trust, passion, and shared ownership.

Systems are the silent scaffolding that hold the dream up. From lean operations and ethical growth to small-scale automation and thoughtful delegation, each decision becomes a brick in a larger structure that supports balance. You begin by carrying the weight yourself, but with time and intention, you distribute that weight across capable shoulders.

And as you do, you find room—room to think, to breathe, to live.

The future of entrepreneurship lies not in working harder, but in building smarter. Not in chasing everything, but in choosing wisely. The ability to adapt quickly, embrace technology, nurture your team, and listen deeply—these are not just survival skills; they are growth accelerators. And balance, then, becomes not a pause or a reward, but a natural by-product of a well-designed life.

As I look back, I realize that balance doesn't mean working less—it means working well. With direction, with systems, with people you trust, and with an inner compass that doesn't waver with every market swing. It's not just a business goal, it's a life philosophy.

"Burnout happens when purpose is absent. But when your 'why' is stronger than any obstacle, you don't burn out—you burn steady."

Ultimately, the goal isn't to dim your ambition for the sake of balance. It's to channel it in a way that allows you to build sustainably, live fully, and glow long after the grind has ended. Balance is not the enemy of growth. It's the foundation of enduring success.

Conclusion

"We make a living by what we get, but we make a life by what we give."

— Winston Churchill

Every great journey has a defining moment when the traveler pauses to look back, not just at how far they have come, but at what they have learned along the way. This book has been an exploration of the entrepreneurial path—not as a race, but as a carefully paced expedition requiring patience, strategy, integrity, and a deep sense of purpose.

Perhaps you remember the story of the entrepreneur who faced repeated failures before their venture found its footing, a reminder that success is rarely immediate but rather a product of careful planning, perseverance, and resilience. This journey is not just about financial gain but about crafting a lasting impact through ethical leadership, sound decision-making, and a well-balanced life.

As we conclude, let's reflect on the key lessons from this book—lessons that will serve as guiding principles as you navigate your own entrepreneurial path.

Patience as a Strategic Advantage

In today's fast-paced business world, instant gratification often masquerades as success. However, patience remains one of the greatest strategic advantages an entrepreneur can possess. Throughout this book, we have explored how patience enables a deeper understanding of the market, facilitates better decision-making, and empowers individuals to weather challenges without compromising their long-term goals.

Rushing to scale a business without a solid foundation can lead to complications, inefficiencies, and burnout. The most impactful companies are not built overnight but through steady, thoughtful growth. By pacing your entrepreneurial journey for sustainability rather than speed, you ensure long-term viability, resilience, and meaningful success.

The health of a business is closely tied to the well-being of its leader. Throughout this book, we have seen how managing stress, expectations, and personal well-being is not just beneficial but essential for long-term success. A fatigued, overworked leader cannot make sound decisions, inspire a team, or drive a company forward effectively. Success is not just about reaching a destination—it's about sustaining the journey without sacrificing personal happiness, relationships, and mental health. Establishing boundaries, practicing mindfulness, and maintaining a work-life balance are not luxuries but necessities.

The Competitive Edge of Integrity and Ethical Leadership

A culture of honesty is a business's greatest asset in building lasting relationships. Trust and transparency are no longer optional in today's world—they are fundamental to success. A business that upholds ethical practices will not only attract loyal customers but will also foster a strong, accountable workplace culture.

Ethical leadership extends beyond compliance; it is about actively doing right by employees, customers, and society. Integrity in competition leads to a more stable and robust business ecosystem, and the trust earned through ethical practices can become one of the most valuable assets for a company. In a world where transparency is increasingly demanded, ethics can serve as a powerful differentiator.

Every entrepreneur must eventually face a critical decision: when and how to transition leadership. Effective succession planning is essential for the long-term success of any business. Recognizing the right time to step down is a sign of strong leadership, not weakness.

Mentorship plays a key role in ensuring that a company's legacy and values endure. The most effective leaders do not simply instruct; they guide, empower, and prepare the next generation to lead with confidence and vision. Leadership development is not a one-time investment but an ongoing process that strengthens the foundation of any business.

Entrepreneurship and Philanthropy: A Synergistic Relationship

Business success and philanthropy are not mutually exclusive; they can coexist. Some of the world's most respected entrepreneurs have leveraged their success to create meaningful change. Giving back—whether through financial contributions, mentorship, or community engagement—builds a legacy that extends beyond personal achievements.

Entrepreneurs hold a unique opportunity to drive societal progress. Strategic, targeted philanthropy amplifies the impact of a business, ensuring that success is not measured merely in revenue but in the lives positively affected.

The Enduring Pursuit of Balance and Compassion

Work-life balance is not a static goal but an ongoing pursuit. The entrepreneurial journey is demanding, but sustainable success requires constant recalibration. Strategies exist to help manage responsibilities without neglecting personal well-being. Awareness, intentionality, and flexibility are key to maintaining balance amid ever-changing demands.

Compassion, both within a business and in the broader community, is a powerful tool. It shapes company culture, strengthens relationships, and enhances reputation. Businesses that lead with compassion not only achieve financial success but also contribute to societal well-being, proving that profitability and positive impact can go hand in hand.

Reflection is a crucial tool for entrepreneurs. Learning from both successes and failures builds resilience, adaptability, and continuous improvement. In an ever-evolving business landscape, the ability to pivot, learn, and grow determines long-term success.

Planning for the future with an ethical compass ensures a legacy that transcends financial achievements. The most successful entrepreneurs are those who remain curious, open to change, and committed to lifelong learning. The entrepreneurial journey does not end with financial milestones—it extends to the impact it leaves on the world.

A Call to Action: What Comes Next?

As you turn the final page of this book, take a moment to reflect on your own journey. Consider the lessons shared and how they apply to your business, leadership, and life. More importantly, take action.

- **Pause and assess:** Where are you in your entrepreneurial journey? What aspects of patience, ethics, balance, and foresight need refinement?
- **Implement one change:** Whether it's setting clearer work boundaries, dedicating time to mentorship, adopting a more ethical business practice, or developing a strategy for long-term adaptability—commit to making a meaningful shift.
- **Stay intentional:** Success is not accidental. It is the result of thoughtful choices, ethical leadership, and sustained effort.

Approach your journey with a sense of purpose and a commitment to long-term impact.

The path of entrepreneurship is not just about reaching an end goal; it is about how you navigate the journey. Lead with patience, integrity, and compassion, and success will follow—not just in business but in the legacy you leave behind.

Entrepreneurship is not a destination; it is an evolving journey. Every challenge overcome, every lesson learned, and every decision made contributes to a greater story—one that extends beyond financial success to the very heart of impact, purpose, and legacy.

So, as you move forward, remember: the greatest businesses are not just built on strategies, numbers, or revenue. They are built on resilience, vision, and an unwavering commitment to creating something that lasts. And that journey—your journey—is just beginning.

Now, go forth and build with patience, lead with integrity, and leave a legacy that matters.

About the author

Navdeep Chawla is an entrepreneur, industry leader, and philanthropist with over four decades of experience in the pharmaceutical sector. Born in Fazilka, Punjab, he was raised in a family deeply rooted in Arya Samaj values. His father, Sh. V.N. Chawla dedicated over 45 years to the DAV Educational Institutions, instilling in him a commitment to discipline, ethics, and lifelong learning.

Chawla's entrepreneurial journey began with a small printing press immediately after graduating from DAV College, Jalandhar, in 1976. However, his career took a significant turn when he joined CIBA-GEIGY in 1978, where he honed his expertise in pharmaceutical sales. After nearly a decade in the corporate world, he took a bold step in 1986 by founding PIL (Psychotropics India Ltd.)

From its humble beginnings, the company has grown into a major pharmaceutical enterprise, with state-of-the-art WHO GMP-approved manufacturing units in Haridwar and operations spanning over 50 countries.

Psychotropics India Ltd. has established itself as a formidable player in India's fast-growing generic drugs market. As of 2023–2024, the company operates across twelve states with an impressive turnover exceeding ₹294 crores.

Beyond business, Chawla has played an active role in industrial and social leadership. As the Past President of the Faridabad Industry Association (2014-2017), he represented the interests of the region's large industrial base.

He has also held key positions in various educational and charitable institutions, including the DAV College Managing Committee, Manav Rachna International University, and the Rotary Club of NCR Golfers.

Recognized for his contributions to industry and society, he was conferred a PhD by Manav Rachna University, Faridabad in the year 2024. He also holds the title of Professor of Practice in the Department of Pharmacy at DAV University, Jalandhar.

Philanthropy is at the heart of Chawla's mission. His family actively supports multiple charitable dispensaries, provides free medicines, and has contributed significantly to healthcare initiatives. One of his most impactful projects includes the renovation of Arya Samaj, Sector-15, Faridabad, and the establishment of a multi-specialty health center in memory of his parents. He has also donated ₹5 crores to the Rotary Foundation, joining the prestigious Arch Klumph Society in Trustee Circle to support global humanitarian efforts, including polio eradication.

A firm believer in ethical business practices, Chawla has built his career on the principles of trust, patience, and long-term vision. His experiences—both successes and challenges—serve as the foundation of this book, where he shares invaluable insights on sustainable entrepreneurship, ethical competition, and the art of passing on a legacy.

With a wealth of real-world experience, Navdeep Chawla is not just an entrepreneur but a mentor and thought leader, guiding the next generation towards building businesses that are not only profitable but also principled and enduring.